PROUD TO PLAY

Canadian LGBTQ+ athletes who made history

Erin Silver

PROUD TO PLAY

Canadian LGBTQ+ athletes who made history

Erin Silver

ERIN SILVER

James Lorimer & Company Ltd., Publishers
Toronto

James Lorimer & Company Ltd., Publishers acknowledges funding support from the Ontario Arts Council (OAC), an agency of the Government of Ontario. We acknowledge the support of the Canada Council for the Arts, which last year invested $153 million to bring the arts to Canadians throughout the country. This project has been made possible in part by the Government of Canada and with the support of Ontario Creates.

Cover design: Gwen North
Cover image: Canadian speedskater Anastasia Bucsis competes at the Speed Skating Single Distance Championships in Calgary, AB, 2009. Photo: THE CANADIAN PRESS/Jeff McIntosh

Back cover: Courtesy of Mark Tewskbury (top); courtesy of Chris Voth, photo by Francois Laplante/Freestyle Photography (second from top); courtesy of Jessica Platt, photo by Lori Bolliger (second from bottom); courtesy of Rose Cossar, photo by Adam Pulicicchio (bottom)

Library and Archives Canada Cataloguing in Publication

Silver, Erin, 1983–, author.
Title: Proud to play : Canadian LGBTQ+ athletes who made history / Erin Silver.
Names: Silver, Erin, 1980- author.
Description: Includes index.
Identifiers: Canadiana 20190186526 | ISBN 9781459415126 (softcover)
Subjects: LCSH: Gay athletes—Canada—Biography—Juvenile literature. | LCSH: Lesbian athletes—Canada—Biography—Juvenile literature. | LCSH: Transgender athletes—Canada—Biography—Juvenile literature. | LCSH: Gays and sports—Canada—Juvenile literature. | LCSH: Lesbians and sports—Canada—Juvenile literature.
Classification: LCC GV708.8 .S55 2021 | DDC j796.086/640922—dc23

Published by:
James Lorimer & Company Ltd., Publishers
117 Peter Street, Suite 304
Toronto, ON, Canada
M5V 0M3
www.lorimer.ca

Distributed in Canada by:
Formac Lorimer Books
5502 Atlantic Street
Halifax, NS, Canada
B3H 1G4

Printed and bound in Canada.

CONTENTS

INTRODUCTION 7

1 **MARK TEWKSBURY**
CANADA'S 1ST OUT OLYMPIC CHAMPION 9

2 **ANASTASIA BUCSIS**
STANDING UP, STANDING TALL 19

3 **ROSIE COSSAR**
WON'T BE JUDGED 29

4 **ERIC RADFORD**
OUT AND PROUD ON THE PODIUM 37

5 **BAXTER AND LYE**
TWO COACHES, TWO DIFFERENT EXPERIENCES 47

6 **CINDY OUELLET**
FEMALE, GAY AND PARALYMPIAN 57

7 **JAMES AND OUELLETTE**
CHANGING TIMES IN WOMEN'S HOCKEY 65

8 **CHRIS VOTH**
CANADA'S 1ST OPENLY GAY MALE ATHLETE ON A NATIONAL TEAM 73

9 **JESSICA PLATT**
THE 1ST OPENLY TRANSGENDER ATHLETE IN CANADIAN
PROFESSIONAL HOCKEY 79

10 **BROCK MCGILLIS**
THE BIG FOUR AND "LOCKER ROOM" CULTURE 89

TIMELINE 95

GLOSSARY 99

ACKNOWLEDGEMENTS 104

PHOTO CREDITS 105

INDEX 107

Introduction

Have you ever had to keep a secret? The kind of secret so big you were afraid to tell anybody? The kind of secret so huge you were afraid *not* to tell, because keeping it to yourself was making it hard to live your life?

This book is about the secrets kept by some of Canada's most elite athletes — and what happened when they told their truth to the world. The stories in this book belong to sports professionals, athletes, Olympians and gold medallists who worked hard and achieved elite levels in their sports. But sometimes they didn't achieve what they wanted, or what they could have, because they didn't feel safe or comfortable competing in the sport they loved. Sometimes they felt so unhappy while reaching for their goals that they thought about giving up.

What were they hiding? Each athlete in this book suffered because they were afraid to admit they were lesbian, gay, bisexual, transgender, queer, or questioning — that they were part of the LGBTQ+ community. Growing up, they had no role models to look up to. Nobody to tell them they could be gay or transgender and succeed in the sport they loved. They knew their lives would be judged by everyone. Would people discriminate against them? Would judges deduct marks? Would coaches cut them from teams? Because of the laws and attitudes at the time, the culture of their respective sports and their very real fears, the athletes in *Proud to Play* kept their secrets from everyone. It wasn't fair. Nobody should have to feel ashamed of themselves or to live in fear.

You are about to read the stories of a handful of Canadians who are brave beyond measure. They came out. They took a stand. They told the world they were proud of themselves. Some helped change the culture of sports in Canada. They never gave in and they never gave up. Instead, they became role models. They teach us through their example what it means to be a real champion.

Thanks to each person in this book, society is changing and the sports world is becoming more welcoming for LGBTQ+ athletes, coaches and even fans. But there is still more work to do to make sports inclusive. By reading this book, you are part of this change, and can help make even more change through action. I hope you will find these stories as inspiring to read as they were for me to write. Together, we can make sports better for everyone.

— Erin Silver

MARK TEWKSBURY

born February 7, 1968, in Calgary, Alberta

CAREER HIGHLIGHTS

- 1988 Seoul Olympics: 100-metre backstroke, 5th place

- 1988 Seoul Olympics: 200-metre backstroke, 12th place

- 1988 Seoul Olympics: 4x100-metre medley relay, silver

- 1992 Barcelona Olympics: 4x100-metre medley relay, bronze

- 1992 Barcelona Olympics: 100-metre backstroke, gold

- Mentor, author, public speaker, and activist

- Media commentator and analyst for the Canadian Broadcasting Corporation (CBC): 2004, 2008, and 2016 Olympic Games

- Has received 5 honorary degrees, the Queen's Jubilee Silver Medal, the Meritorious Service Medal, and a Muhammad Ali Humanitarian Award for Gender Equality

1
MARK TEWKSBURY
Canada's 1st Out Olympic Champion

When Mark Tewksbury was young, he loved spending summers with his grandmother. His parents would bus him from their home in Calgary to visit her at her condo in Lethbridge, Alberta. Mark already knew how to swim, but it was in his grandmother's pool at age seven that he learned to love it. In fact, he loved the water as much as he loved being wrapped from head-to-toe in a big, fluffy towel afterward. Watching the 1976 Summer Olympics on TV inspired him to become a champion.

Tewksbury worked hard to achieve his goal. By 1982, when Mark was 14, he even had to stop visiting his grandmother to focus on swimming. It was also at that age that other boys started talking about girls — dating them, wanting to have sex with them. Tewksbury began to understand that he wasn't interested in the same way. He was thinking about boys. But Mark knew he had to keep his thoughts to himself.

Already, kids were picking on him at school. They called him "fag" and "gay," even though he didn't understand exactly what *gay* meant. All Mark knew was that the words were used to hurt him and make him feel bad.

As a young man, Mark Tewksbury proved he had the potential to be a champion in the pool.

"I became a loner," Mark wrote in his autobiography, *Inside Out: Straight Talk from a Gay Jock*. "I hated going to school. I constantly felt like a loser."

Every day, Mark worried someone would attack him just because he was different. To stay safe, he got to school right on time, ate lunch at home and ran off at the end of the day to swim. But his plan wasn't foolproof. One day in grade eight, he got to school to discover someone had broken into his locker. When he opened the locker door, he saw the word *fag* had been written in black ink on one of his binders. In that moment, Tewksbury was filled with rage. But no matter how much someone else hated him, he hated himself more. His locker destroyed, Tewksbury ran home. His parents were horrified when he told them what had happened. The next day, when the principal suggested Mark change schools, Mark's parents let him. Tewksbury hoped for a fresh start, but trouble followed him to the next school, too.

"My freedom, my fresh start, had lasted less than two days before it came crashing down around me," he wrote. "Where whispers in hallways had followed me before, now the attacks and discrimination were a full-on daily assault."

The only place Mark felt accepted was at the University of Calgary pool. His swimming improved each year and he was celebrated for his achievements. It was the one place he excelled. He trained even harder. Mark promised himself he would become the best swimmer. He also swore he would do anything to keep his sexuality a secret. The consequences were too great to let people know — his swimming career was at stake. It was the beginning of his double life.

"I was at a place where I didn't care anymore. I had to be me."

At his first Olympics in Seoul, South Korea, in 1988, Mark helped his 4x100-metre relay team win a silver medal. He kept training. By the time he was 24, Tewksbury made it to the 1992 Summer Olympics in Barcelona, Spain. He had worked so hard, kept so many secrets. As he waited for his race to start, he knew that this race — the 100-metre backstroke — would decide whether all the pain and sacrifice were worth it.

Mark stood as his name was announced over the loudspeaker. He adjusted his goggles, took a deep breath and shook out his muscles, mentally preparing for the race of a lifetime. Everyone in Canada knew his name. The hopes of a nation rested on his broad shoulders. In lane five, between his two biggest rivals, Mark took his starting position in the water, gripping the bar along the edge of the pool.

As the mechanical beep sounded, there wasn't a nano-second to waste. Mark flung himself into the water, kicking, kicking, kicking. Finally, he popped up about halfway down

HOMOPHOBIA IN SPORT

How common is it to be bullied in youth sport? It's a major problem, according to a 2015 report called *Out on the Fields* — the first international study on homophobia in sport. In Canada, 86 per cent of participants saw homophobia; 53 per cent experienced it themselves. The most common forms were insults and slurs, such as "fag" or "dyke." Phrases like, "that's so gay," and gay jokes were also common. The most likely place for homophobia to happen is in the stands and in school gym classes. Eighty-four per cent of people in the study said homophobic jokes and humour occur "all the time," "often" or "sometimes." Only one per cent thought lesbian, gay and bisexual (LGB) people were "completely accepted" in sports.

Mark beat his personal best time by more than 1.2 seconds to win the 100-metre backstroke.

the pool and kept swimming hard. The swimmers propelled themselves toward the other end. The country held its breath.

At that time, Mark was ranked fourth in the world. He was the underdog behind American world record–holder Jeff Rouse. But Mark was strong and determined. Could he do it?

Mark forged his way through the water. The TV commentator was excited as Mark touched off the wall at the 50-metre mark in second place. "He's ahead of the other American, a little bit weak off the turn there . . ."

The drama continued in real-time. "Mark has to play catch up again, but he's good at that — he's got to pick it up now!"

Fans rose to their feet. The commentator screamed, "Here comes Mark Tewksbury, to the final five metres! It's gonna go to the wall! And on the wall — history! Tewksbury! He's done it! Olympic record!"

Mark won Olympic gold in 1992 by six one-hundredths of a second.

Mark broke the surface of the water. His mouth fell open in shock as his name blinked first on the scoreboard. Holding his head in disbelief, he flashed the world a big smile. He jumped and screamed in the water. Mark had passed Jeff Rouse on the last stroke of the race to capture gold by six one-hundredths of a second, beating his personal best time by more than 1.2 seconds.

That gold was Canada's first in Barcelona and its first swimming gold since the 1984 Olympics. It made Mark Tewksbury famous. His face appeared on the cover of *Time* magazine. He was inducted into the Canadian Olympic Hall of Fame, the Canadian Sports Hall of Fame and the International Swimming Hall of Fame. He was also named Canada's Male Athlete of the Year for 1992. After the Games, Mark retired from swimming. He criss-crossed the country giving motivational talks. He wrote a book, and got several endorsement deals.

But fame changed everything for Mark Tewksbury. Suddenly, he was an Olympic champion — the very image of the perfect male athlete. He remembered how disgusted people were when they thought he was gay in high school. What would everyone think now if they knew he was gay?

"I thought my agent would be someone I could navigate this with," he said in an interview for the podcast *Player's Own Voice.* "But my agent wanted to keep the gay quiet because it would counter the fame."

As Mark explained, there was a "morality clause" in every contract he signed. In 1992, being gay could make him responsible for harming a sponsor's image or reputation.

Mark became depressed. This should have been the time of his life. Instead, his secret made life too hard. To escape the pressure, Mark moved to Australia. He studied sport and sexuality. He became more comfortable with himself. When he returned to Canada, he felt stronger and more empowered.

He would need this strength for what happened next.

In December 1998, Mark was told he was "too gay" and lost a major public speaking deal. At the time, he was still in the closet, hiding that he was gay. But losing that deal changed everything. He'd had enough.

GOLD MEDAL DROP

One time the *National Post* newspaper asked Mark Tewksbury who was the most memorable person to have held his gold medal. Mark answered with a laugh: "Well, it's been dropped three times. And I'll never forget the first time it was dropped. It was just a young girl, probably six or seven years old. And everyone was horrified. Everyone looked to me . . . I just smiled. I actually think that little dent gives the medal way more character."

Winning gold made Mark famous. At the time, nobody knew he was gay.

"I was tired of walking away from it," Mark said. "I was already paying the consequences, so I figured I might as well face it. I was at a place where I didn't care anymore. I had to be me."

Mark made it official. He told the world he was gay.

He thought the news might be buried in the back of the sports section. Instead, his announcement made front-page news at home and around the world. In the 1990s, there were few openly gay role models in sport. Mark Tewksbury became Canada's first out male Olympic champion. "It was a strange period," Mark said. "It was hugely freeing — the beginning of many more years of getting to know myself." But it was also a struggle. "My parents took it very badly. My father died without accepting me for who I was."

What Mark had wanted all along was to be accepted by his family, teammates, coaches and sponsors. But in sport, being gay and accepted was almost impossible.

"Sport is homophobic. It's traditional, rule-bound, run by old white guys and driven by commercial mentality," Mark explained. "Elementary and high schools are better, but at higher levels, it's difficult to be openly gay in a team sport. At some point, we end up with

On the 20th anniversary of his coming out, Mark created and performed a one-man play, *Belong*, which projected footage of him swimming on screen while he performed on stage.

homogeneous teams where standing out for any reason isn't encouraged. And swimming is actually a team sport — it's impossible to be a swimmer without the support of your team. It's really tough."

Swimming also has something other sports don't always have: sex appeal. A swimmer's body is smooth and muscular. To be fast in the water and reduce friction, they wear the smallest swimsuits possible. With athletes exposed and on display, "it's very sexual," said Mark.

It's common for athletes to make homophobic comments about gay people in locker rooms. It makes gay athletes want to stay in the closet, to hide their sexual orientation, until they've retired. It makes some not want to come out at all.

For Mark, living and competing in the closet was hard. "The sense of isolation and loneliness was so intense when I felt like I was the only one. There was no internet back then. It was hard to know I wasn't alone."

Since Mark came out, more than 20 years ago, there's been a lot of progress. But Mark saw the biggest change as being society. "In general, there's so much more awareness, communication and language that didn't exist [when I was] growing up."

Mark Tewksbury has been one of the change-makers. He's used his fame to make sports more welcoming for all athletes. In 2006, he was president of the first World OutGames in Montreal, a big sporting event hosted by the gay community. Two years later, he spoke at the United Nations when they wanted to reverse laws that made it a crime to be gay. As a director of the Canadian Olympic Committee, he fights for fair and inclusive rules for athletes. Mark is also involved with Special Olympics Canada, where he supports athletes with intellectual disabilities.

Canada's first out male Olympian is also a mentor and role model. He often speaks at high schools and to young athletes. He shares his painful personal experiences to teach kids it's not okay to pick on someone because they are different in some way.

For all his achievements, Mark has received several honorary degrees and awards. For instance, the University of Western Ontario awarded him with an honorary Doctorate of Laws. He also received an honorary degree from the University of Calgary.

As the *Toronto Star* wrote, "Only the greatest fight for what they believe in, taking on people and institutions and closed minds, because the battle is important. Few have done that more often, more successfully, and more importantly than Tewksbury."

THE OLYMPICS ARE FOR EVERYONE

The Olympic Games is the largest, most famous sporting event in the world. Every four years, thousands of athletes from more than 200 countries compete. The Winter and Summer Games alternate, so every two years there is a Winter or Summer Olympics. The modern games were inspired by the ancient Olympic Games, held in Olympia, Greece, from the eighth century BCE to the fourth century CE. The first modern Games took place in Athens, Greece, in 1896. Since then, several other Games have been created, including the Paralympic Games for athletes with a disability.

With the #OneTeam initiative, the Canadian Olympic Committee (COC) partners with the organizations You Can Play and Egale Canada to make the Olympics more welcoming for all athletes. They are committed to protecting LGBTQ+ rights at other levels of sport, too. Ambassadors for #OneTeam visit schools and talk to young athletes about mental health and equality in sport to change attitudes on the field, off the field and in the locker room. Their goal is to ensure everyone from amateur athletes to coaches and fans feels safe and welcome in sport.

ANASTASIA BUCSIS

born April 30, 1989, in Calgary, Alberta

CAREER HIGHLIGHTS

- 2010 Vancouver Olympics: 500-metre long track speed skating, 23rd place (overall)

- International Skating Union World Single Distances Championships, 2011: 20th place (500-metre); 2012: 15th place (500-metre); 2013: 19th place (500-metre), 18th place (1,000-metre)

- 2014 Sochi Olympics: 500-metre long track speed skating, 27th place

- 46 World Cup starts overall

- Host of CBC podcast, *Player's Own Voice*

- Degree in Communications from the University of Calgary

- Appeared in a 2019 documentary about homophobia in sports, *Standing on the Line*

2

ANASTASIA BUCSIS
Standing Up, Standing Tall

Anastasia Bucsis was born in Calgary a year after the city hosted the 1988 Winter Olympics. Everyone was still excited about the success of the Olympic Games and were proud of the new world-class facilities that had been built for the big event.

When she was four years old, Anastasia wanted to try gymnastics and figure skating. Because she was tall for her age, her parents, Ross and Anita, thought she should try speed skating instead. They took their daughter to skate at the Calgary Olympic Oval. By the time she was seven, Anastasia had the chance to skate with two of her Olympic heroes, Catriona Le May Doan and Susan Auch. These Olympic speed skaters inspired Anastasia to work toward competing at the Olympics, too. The Oval became her home. She worked very hard as she grew up, training six to eight hours a day, six days a week.

But inside her heart, Anastasia was sad. She knew she was gay and liked girls, but she was afraid to tell anyone. What would her parents, her friends, her teammates and her coaches think if they knew? "It makes me embarrassed and ashamed to admit that I didn't want to be gay, but being born and raised in a very conservative and Catholic family, I was

Anastasia Bucsis ✓
@anastasure

[Follow] ⌄

Great day. If you can play, you can play.
#Pride2018

1:47 PM - 24 Jun 2018

40 Retweets 549 Likes

Brian Burke, Kate Pettersen, Korey Jarvis and PiperGilles

💬   ↻ 40   ♡ 549

Anastasia (left) frequently shares her support of fellow LGBTQ+ athletes, initiatives, and allies on social media.

incredibly ignorant, alone, and afraid," Anastasia wrote later in a blog post for the Student-Athlete Mental Health Initiative (SAMHI). "I had absolutely nothing 'alternative' in my life, and certainly no gay friends to connect to. I felt a loneliness that didn't leave . . ."

Anastasia's once-cheerful personality was destroyed by fear. She had panic attacks, and suffered from anxiety and depression, all because she hated feeling different. "I wanted to live a 'normal,' white-picket-fence life, and as I was so alone and confused, I didn't know how I could happily live while being gay."

But she kept skating and had a breakout year in 2009. By the age of 20, Anastasia had qualified for the 2010 Olympics. She was part of the strongest Canadian speed skating team ever. She travelled the world, made good friends and trained with skating legends. Everyone thought she could win.

Then…disappointment. All the feelings she felt off the ice followed her onto the ice, too. Anastasia placed 34th in her event at the Vancouver Games. "When I had a good race, my smile didn't touch my eyes; when I skated poorly, I would rather have been dead," she wrote for CBC Sports. "I attached all of my self-worth to my results — further eroding my mental health and my love for sport."

SUICIDE AND LGBTQ+ YOUTH

Statistics Canada research shows that approximately 500 Canadian young people (ages 10 to 24) die by suicide each year. Many studies confirm that suicidal thoughts and behaviour are more common among LGBTQ+ youth. One study found that 33 per cent of LGB youth have attempted suicide, compared to seven per cent of youth in general. In another study, over half of LGB students (47 per cent of gay/bisexual males and 73 per cent of lesbian/bisexual females) have thought about suicide. Research also shows a big link between being rejected by family and increased rates of suicide and depression. Support from parents and peers can make a world of difference to a young LGB person.

Instead of enjoying competing, she could only focus on the results — results often decided by one one-thousandth of a second. "Regardless of my placing or time, I would cross the finish line hating myself; knowing full well that the work I had put in was never going to be enough to cure my cancerous lack of self-love." It was the emptiest feeling in the world.

By 2011, Anastasia couldn't hide anymore. She came out to her parents. It was a huge relief when her mother, Anita, said, "We're here to love, not judge." Her family, friends, sponsors, coaches and teammates supported her, too. They wanted her to be herself. They loved her no matter what.

Anastasia was lucky. As she grew up, she'd known many athletes who dropped out of sport because they were gay. She could have dropped out, too. But she didn't.

Anastasia was aware that it was the little comments or jokes that made some athletes feel so uncomfortable they didn't want to participate: "People don't understand the power of language. It's so habitual. They might say, 'that's so gay,' or make a joke that's a slight on someone's orientation. People can be ignorant — these are insults that derail [a person's] mental health. It's what keeps kids in the closet, and why we see disproportionate rates of suicide among LGBTQ youth."

Anastasia Bucsis

"I would regret it for the rest of my life if I didn't stand up for what I believed in."

Thanks to Anastasia and other athletes, things are changing. "We still have a long way to go, but we are making leaps and bounds to eliminate homophobic language in sport," she said. "We're changing who's accepted, so everyone feels like sport is a safe place. We need to be aware of what we're saying and how we're treating people. Sport is for everyone."

While she didn't have any openly gay speed skaters to talk to at the time, Anastasia found a role model and friend in Mark Tewksbury. An Olympic gold-medal swimmer who is also gay, Tewksbury encouraged Anastasia to be proud of herself. This was great advice, especially since she was headed to Sochi, Russia, to compete in the 2014 Winter Games.

As the Sochi Olympics neared, new laws were passed in Russia that made it harder for gay people to live freely. Anastasia decided she had to come out more publicly. She wanted to tell the world what she thought about those laws. They were wrong! Anastasia made her announcement at the 2013 Calgary Pride Parade. "Coming out was the right thing for me to do," she said. "It was a very personal decision, but I knew I would regret it for the rest of my life if I didn't stand up for what I believed in."

Anastasia got a lot of media attention after her announcement. Only a handful of openly gay athletes were competing in Russia, and Anastasia was the only one from North America. Reaction to her announcement was mixed. "Some people from the athletic community said, 'We support you, but you don't need to talk about it,'" she said. "Meanwhile, the LGBTQ community wanted me to speak more and do more than I did."

Anastasia (top row, sixth from the right) is a #OneTeam ambassador for the Canadian Olympic Committee.

A HOCKEY MVP?

In 2014, Anastasia Bucsis got to compete at the same Olympic Games as her then-girlfriend, Canadian hockey superstar Charline Labonté. The night the Canadian women's hockey team won the gold medal, Anastasia became the team's unofficial MVP. As Labonté tells it: "Following this amazing gold-medal game, we celebrated with our families and friends. Anastasia was nowhere to be found. It was almost 1:00 a.m., so I figured she was just too tired to celebrate. Minutes later, she returned with a big bag . . . In the bag were 50 cheeseburgers and 50 packets of Chicken McNuggets. She had ridden her bike to the McDonald's in the Olympic Village! Our team played a fantastic game that night, but right then and there, Anastasia was our MVP."

Anastasia didn't go to the Games to protest. She was there to be the best athlete she could be. She ended up placing 27th in the 500-metre. "Lending my face and my name meant that kids who needed to hear my message would hear it," she said.

For many athletes, Sochi was a turning point. "When the world comes together, we need to ask, what can we do to make it a better place?" said Anastasia. "The Olympics shows our similarities outweigh our differences."

In 2017, Anastasia retired from sport because of a knee injury that wouldn't heal. She was disappointed her skating career ended early, but she had accomplished a lot by age 27. By then, Anastasia had 46 World Cup starts and she had competed in six World Championships and two Olympic Games.

Most importantly, Anastasia took control of her depression. She asked for help. As she wrote for SAMHI, "Going on medication was mentally and physically a struggle, but with time, I started to gradually improve. Medication didn't provide me with all the answers to life, but it gave me a quiet calm that allowed me to eventually start living in the direction I intended to."

Since getting help, Anastasia has gone off medication. She is taking good care of herself. "I try to always stay on top of my sleep, surround myself with people that are uplifting, and take time to recharge and maintain an internal calm," she said.

Anastasia wants people to feel comfortable talking about depression and mental illness so they can get the help they need. She wishes she had reached out sooner. "If I would have had the wherewithal to ask for help earlier, I would have not only been happier off of the ice, but I would have been a stronger skater on it as well . . . I am begging you, if you are feeling depressed, or alone, or confused, to ask for help."

She wants everyone to get the message: "We all struggle. We all have problems. Regardless of fame, money, or success, we all have our individual issues that are made better through reaching out and asking for help."

In addition to supporting mental health causes, Anastasia is a #OneTeam ambassador and talks to kids across the country about her experience as an LGBTQ+ athlete. She is also involved with You Can Play, a non-profit organization that aims to end homophobia in sport. She hopes that sharing all sides of her story will help others know they're not alone.

Even though she is no longer skating full-time, she is still involved in sports. With a degree in Communications from the University of Calgary, Anastasia works for CBC Sports as a broadcaster. She hosts a podcast called *Player's Own Voice*. "I love telling stories and being a broadcaster," she said. "It's an extension of my own heart and interests."

Sugar Todd and Anastasia after their heat in the 500-metre at the 2014 Sochi Olympics.

Anastasia Bucsis

"We're changing who's accepted, so everyone feels like sport is a safe place."

Anastasia has interviewed Mark Tewksbury about being a gay athlete. She has interviewed legendary Team Canada hockey player Caroline Ouellette about having a baby with her partner, American hockey Olympian Julie Chu. She even interviewed Brian Burke, co-founder of You Can Play, about homophobia in hockey and how it's changing.

By being visible and talking openly about mental health and homophobia in sports, Anastasia is making a difference. "Even if you are in an individual sport, life is a team effort . . . Love yourself, and love one another, because at the end of the day, that's all that really matters."

Scott MacArthur — Talks the Talk

Scott MacArthur spent his career trying to be the best sportscaster he could be. As he rose through the ranks at local radio and TV networks, then at TSN and Sportsnet, his career became all-consuming. "I worked so many hours for so many days covering the Blue Jays between 2013 and 2015 for the full 162-game schedule," said Scott. "I'd go seven to eight months without two days off in a row."

That left no time in his life for relationships, to get married or have a family. But as he approached 40, Scott felt burnt out. "I realized I was using work as my shield," he said.

All this time, he was trying to hide from the fact he was gay. It wasn't society holding him back. It was nothing anyone had ever said. He wasn't afraid of what his parents would think if they knew. They had always been supportive of everything he and his brother ever did. "It was my own inability to accept myself." Scott was raised in the small suburb of Oakville, Ontario. "As I grew up [in the] 1990s, there was no homophobia, because as far as I knew there was no homosexuality."

But by age 12 or 13, Scott started to feel different. He no longer wanted to hang out with the friends he'd had all his life. He couldn't figure out what was wrong. When he realized he was attracted to men, he assumed it was a phase that would pass. But it never did.

"I developed assumptions and beliefs about myself that I carried into young adulthood and into my 30s that I didn't want to be gay," he explained. "I wanted to be straight. I convinced myself with good intention that the next accomplishment in my life surely would change me — a new job, promotion, or raise. When you are desperate to change, you can convince yourself the impossible is possible."

By 2015, he couldn't continue living the way he had been. Scott saw a therapist. That's when he finally admitted to himself that he was gay. Next, he told his parents and friends. It took years for him to learn to accept himself.

In 2019, he was feeling strong. Scott came out in a video he posted on social media. The support he received was amazing. "I received about 1,600 replies to my video on Twitter and got hundreds of direct messages on Instagram and Twitter, plus emails, texts and calls. Everyone has been 100 per cent supportive," he said. "I believe not only am I supported, but nobody is even cutting any jokes behind my back about this — people are just happy I'm happy. It has been very rewarding and affirming."

As a man who hid his identity from himself for 25 years, Scott has a message for others: "If you are good to yourself and other people, everything is right and nothing is wrong about you," he said. "We can't control the skin colour, gender identity, or sexual orientation we are born with — it's our nature. Don't deny yourself your nature. If you deny your nature, you deny your person. No good can come from that."

ROSIE COSSAR

born July 4, 1991, in England

CAREER HIGHLIGHTS

- Represented Canada at the 2009, 2010 and 2011 World Rhythmic Gymnastics Championships, the 2011 Pan American Games and the 2012 Summer Olympics

- Captain of Team Canada's women's rhythmic gymnastics team, 2009–12

- 2011 Pan Am Games: team silver (3 ribbons + 2 hoops; all-around) and bronze (5 balls)

- 2012 London Olympics: Women's Rhythmic Group All-Around, 11th place

- Awarded Youth Role Model of the Year in 2017 by *Canadian Centre for Gender and Sexuality* (CCGSD)

- Worked with The 519 to create Pride House Toronto, a resource for LGBTQ+ athletes, during the 2015 Pan American Games

3
ROSIE COSSAR
Won't Be Judged

Rosie Cossar was born in England and moved to Canada when she was a young girl. She began taking gymnastics at the age of five. By the time she was 10, she was competing internationally. Her first competition was called the Happy Cup. But as she grew up and became an expert in her sport, Rosie was anything but happy inside.

While she thrived as an athlete, Rosie was under a lot of stress to hide that she was gay. She feared telling her family or even her closest friends. Rosie knew that her career would be over if anyone found out. This left her feeling alone and afraid.

Why was Rosie so worried?

There were many reasons. Rhythmic gymnastics is known as one of the toughest sports ever invented. These athletes aren't just gymnasts — they are dancers, acrobats and artists. As well as showing the grace and physical strength of their own bodies, they make use of balls, hoops, clubs, ropes or ribbons. In a group performance, five girls or women compete as a team. With their hair pulled back into tight buns, they are made up like dolls, with eyeliner, eyeshadow and blush. Their skin-tight costumes glitter with hundreds of sparkly crystals. When their music begins, they perform a series of leaps, balances and spins.

Rosie roller blading at age 10. She always had a lot of energy, and says she was a lot of work for her parents.

Gymnasts have just two-and-a-half minutes to wow the judges. Each team is under great pressure: judges can take away marks for a range of penalties. Even one mistake can cost an athlete or team the title.

In some countries, being gay is seen as a mistake. Rhythmic gymnastics is beautiful to watch, but it has this ugly side. That's because the sport maintains strong ties to Eastern Europe, part of the world that still has laws against LGBTQ+ people.

"Who am I if I'm not the real me?"

"I spent a lot of time training in Moscow, and homophobia was very high," Rosie said. "My coach considered being gay an illness. She believed gay people needed to be treated the same as someone with a mental illness, in a hospital setting. It wasn't a safe environment, and I knew 100 per cent that it would impact my place on the Canadian team."

With no other options, Rosie started to lie. "I'd pretend I was interested in boys. I'd participate in conversations with my teammates about boys. I knew I wasn't being authentic."

Lying was tiring, and it hurt her mental health. Rosie started to lose herself. "Who am I if I'm not the real me?" she asked herself.

Rosie's struggle at hiding the truth showed through in her performance. Her teammates wondered what her problem was. The stress affected her practices and her ability to push herself past her limit every day. At times, she broke down during training, unable to continue.

But Rosie didn't give up. Instead of quitting, she trained harder. By then, her sport was her life. "When you're doing a sport like gymnastics, you eat, sleep, and breathe it. It was my career. I had opportunities. I was really excelling. I had a drive and determination to keep going no matter how hard it got."

While her mental and physical health suffered, Rosie always found a way to keep going for the team. "People had to trust I'd always deliver."

And her work paid off. By the end of 2011, Rosie's team had qualified for the Olympics. It was a big milestone. The 2012 London Games would be the first time a Canadian team had qualified for the Olympics in the group event. And Rosie was the captain of the team. She was very proud!

But with the Olympics a year away, Rosie suddenly wanted to reveal her secret. "I didn't want to compete unless I was my true self," she said. "It wasn't acceptable to me to hide. I couldn't go to the Olympics if I wasn't representing myself."

Rosie decided to come out, even though she was afraid of how everyone would react.

Her close teammates were supportive. One of her coaches was, too. But some parents of her teammates asked if she was fit to lead the team. They worried about whether she was a good influence on their daughters.

Rosie's Russian coach was very upset. "It was like I told her I had cancer," Rosie said. "Being gay was a disease that needed to be cured. She worried about how I would live my life and raise a family. I don't fault her, because that's the way she was raised in Russia. She didn't understand this was the only way I could be happy."

By then, Rosie's position on the team was safe. She had worked hard to be the best. She was the right athlete to lead the team to the Olympics. The only question now: what would the judges think?

"The next competition we had after I came out, I remember feeling people were re-evaluating me as a person and athlete. People had to reassess me from scratch," Rosie said.

Free of her secret, Rosie's performance improved. "I performed better than I had in my whole life. I didn't make any mistakes. All of a sudden, I was able to bring my full self to practices. It was a total game-changer in my career. I had confidence. I knew what I was doing. I totally believed in myself in a way I never had before."

Everything came together. Rosie said that sharing the spotlight with her team made it easier than competing individually. She felt even stronger after telling her team and the national gymnastics federation about her sexuality. But Rosie didn't come out publicly in the media until 2016, two years after she retired from the sport.

Rosie and her team finished 11th at the 2012 Olympics. "We were the first Canadian team to ever make the Games." And the judging was fair: "What we performed is what we got in terms of marks."

Looking back, Rosie wishes she had a role model in her sport when she was competing. Unfortunately, there was no one. "There wasn't a single rhythmic gymnast who was out during my 16-year career," she said. "There must have been plenty of them, but they were in the closet. I spent my career searching for someone I could look up to. I wanted to know that if they made it, I could, too."

So Rosie decided she needed to be that person for younger athletes. She tries her best to set a good example for others. "I use the drive I had as an athlete to be an advocate and role model," she said. "Sport needs to be more inclusive. I've seen progress and improvement along the way, but I also know what needs to be done and what barriers exist for athletes."

Thanks to Rosie and many other LGBTQ+ athletes and allies (people who support LGBTQ+ rights), a big effort is being made to make sports more inclusive. Rosie finds her work as a #OneTeam ambassador, talking to young people about making sports more inclusive, is especially rewarding.

Rosie Cossar (left) was afraid to come out in a sport where judges can deduct points for even the smallest mistakes.

Rosie proudly marches in the 2014 World Pride Parade with the Canadian Olympic Committee.

"Sharing my story has empowered me and enabled me to help others. In high school, meeting a gay Olympian would have made a world of difference for me; it's been incredible to see that happen for other high school students. They hold my hand and the tears come and you can tell you've made a huge impact."

There's still work to do, especially on the international level. In the meantime, Rosie is focusing on Canada's success so far. "It's so awesome to see us conquer areas and make improvements wherever we can," she said. "We are working together to push the Canadian sport system to a better place."

Kris Burley — Judgement and Acceptance

Only women can compete in rhythmic gymnastics at the Olympic level, but men compete in other kinds of gymnastics. So was life any easier for a gay male gymnast? According to retired Canadian Olympic gymnast Kris Burley, the answer was no.

Kris grew up in Nova Scotia and began doing gymnastics when he was five. The other kids picked on him. "Guys played hockey and girls did gymnastics or figure skating. I was doing an all-girls sport," Kris told *Outsports* magazine. "In fact, I started with an all-girls club because they had no boys club for me. I was teased and bullied when I was in elementary school. That's how I started off in my sport."

While he excelled and even went to the 1996 Summer Olympics, he stayed in the closet the whole time he was on the Canadian National Team. It wasn't safe to come out. Once, a teammate broke Kris's nose so badly that he ended up in hospital. Then, when a teammate did come out, he was treated unfairly — by his own team. "People would constantly make fun of him behind his back. He was kind of shunned in a way. I remember seeing that and thinking 'I don't want that to happen to me' in a judged sport where your reputation is a factor. It was just better to stay in the closet and focus on my performance."

Kris retired from gymnastics in 2000 at age 25 and joined Cirque du Soleil. It was the first time he felt accepted for being gay. Times have changed since he was a competitive athlete, but there is still more work to do until all athletes feel accepted. That's why he is now a #OneTeam ambassador. He is very impressed by athletes like Rosie Cossar, who is a courageous, pioneering athlete brave enough to come out while competing in a judged sport.

ERIC RADFORD

born January 27, 1985, in Winnipeg, Manitoba

CAREER HIGHLIGHTS

- 2014 Sochi Olympics: 7th (pairs), silver (team); 2018 PyeongChang Olympics: bronze (pairs), gold (team)

- International Skating Union (ISU) World Championships, 2011: 7th; 2012: 5th; 2013: bronze; 2014: bronze; 2015: gold; 2016: gold; 2017: 7th

- ISU Four Continents Championships, 2011: silver; 2012: 4th; 2013: gold; 2015: gold; 2017: silver

- ISU Grand Prix Final, 2011: 5th: 2012: 4th; 2013: 5th; 2014: gold; 2015: silver; 2016: bronze

- Co-author, *Soulmates On Ice: From Hometown Glory to Top of the Podium*

- Holds a Grade 9 Royal Conservatory of Music certificate and has composed music for other Canadian athletes

4
ERIC RADFORD
Out and Proud on the Podium

Eric Radford grew up in Balmertown, Ontario, a hockey-crazed town of 1,000 people. As a young child, Eric was picked on because he wanted to be a figure skater when every other boy wanted to play hockey.

"I never could figure out exactly why the other kids would make fun of me for choosing a certain sport," Eric wrote in an article for Sportsnet.

Eric loved skating so much, he kept training, no matter what anyone said. But kids didn't just make fun of him because he was a figure skater. They also made fun of his lisp and teased him for acting "gay." It was very hurtful, so the young skater focused on what he loved. At age 13, Eric moved away from home to skate. This was his chance to reinvent himself. He didn't want to be known as a gay skater. He wanted to be known as a great skater. He learned how to speak without a lisp and became more aware of his mannerisms. And he kept skating. Every year he was in high school, Eric moved to a different city across the country to train. At age 15, he met Paul Wirtz, a great coach and the first out gay man Eric had ever met. The only other gay men he'd seen were on TV. Paul made a positive impact on Eric's skating, and on his life, too. "He made me realize it [being gay] wasn't something to be afraid of," Eric said about his coach.

At age 13, Eric Radford was so committed to skating that he moved away from home to train.

As he got older, Eric switched from individual skating to pairs skating. When he and his pairs partner failed to qualify for the 2010 Olympics, Eric didn't know what to do. He thought maybe he should quit. But then he met fellow figure skater Meagan Duhamel. They became friends and decided to skate together.

Success didn't come easily. Eric and Meagan won a silver medal in the team event at the 2014 Olympic Games, but placed seventh in the pairs event. The duo was very disappointed.

At this time, Eric was at another crossroads. Eric's family, Meagan and the skating community knew he was gay. And now Eric felt the time was right to tell the world. He believed that sharing his story would help him be freer and more confident on the ice. He hoped his performances would improve if he could just be himself. He also wanted to be a role model for other kids.

"I put myself in the position of a young kid who might be afraid to follow their own dream," Eric wrote for Sportsnet. "Or maybe they just want to get out of their own small

Eric Radford and his skating partner Meagan Duhamel are best friends and each other's biggest supporters.

town and do something in the world. If that young kid was able to see someone on TV — someone similar to myself, who was openly gay and winning medals — then maybe that would give them the confidence to feel it was truly possible for them."

Eric came out in December 2014 in *Outsports* magazine. He knew it was the right decision, but he was scared. A million thoughts ran through his mind. How would judges score him: based on his performance or on his sexual orientation? Would sponsors dump him? How would fans react? What if nobody wanted to hire him for skating tours and he couldn't earn a living?

"By speaking out, I could make a difference."

No other athlete had ever come out at the peak of their career. In the last several decades, some athletes had been forced out of the closet. Other athletes shared their secret only after retiring. These athletes worried they would face discrimination by teammates, sponsors, sport governing bodies and the public.

That's what happened to Brian Orser, one of Canada's most famous figure skaters. In 1998, Brian was forced out of the closet during a lawsuit filed by a former partner. Brian was afraid his sexuality would ruin his career and asked the judge to keep his court files private. The two-time Olympic silver medallist lost the case and the court files were released. Suddenly, the world knew he was gay. He was embarrassed. Luckily, the public supported him, and Orser was still able to earn a living as a professional skater and coach.

Eric worried about what people would say when they read his announcement online. "People can be ruthless, and they can create their own idea of you as a person, based on an article," he wrote. "I was worried that it might not unfold the way I had wanted it to in my head."

Eric gathered his courage. He needed to be brave for other kids who were also being bullied. "My fear of coming out wasn't as strong as my desire to get my story out there . . . By speaking out, I could make a difference."

Did he do the right thing? Yes!

Instead of rejection, Eric received support. "The reaction was positive and warm," he said. "I was blown away by messages I got from complete strangers."

Reporters called for interviews. They wanted to help tell his story. At competitions, officials, judges and skaters told Eric he had done a great thing. "In a sport like figure

Champion skater Brian Orser was forced out of the closet in 1998.

skating, I hoped people would be supportive, but cultural differences at the international level were such a big unknown. It caused me a lot of anxiety. I was surprised in the end. I always hoped for the best."

Now that he's older, Eric understands why he was picked on as a kid. "As an adult, I can look back on my childhood and see these kids were bullying me because they really didn't know any better," he said. "It came down to a lack of education. People are afraid of things they don't know much about . . . It made me stronger and it helped me realize what was really important to me: family, friends, and never giving up."

After his announcement, Eric became more confident than ever. Suddenly, he could focus wholly on skating. His skating got even better. He felt lighter and energized. Anything was possible.

But it was still risky. Eric didn't know what would happen at future competitions. That's because, like gymnastics, figure skating is a sport that is scored by judges. There were no guarantees that the judges would be fair.

"It's a scary path to walk for a figure skater," wrote *Outsports*' Cyd Zeigler, author of the article in which Eric came out. "Unlike a sprinter, they are not timed. Unlike a football player, they don't have stats like catches and sacks. A figure skater's success depends on the

Eric and Meagan skated to a bronze medal in the pairs free skate program at the 2018 Olympics, where Eric was the first out competitor to win a gold medal.

subjective scores of judges … An elite international judge won't give a 5 to a 9 performance. But a point here and there?"

As a pairs figure skater, Eric faced an even bigger challenge. Usually skaters use their bodies and music to tell a love story. Just think of how excited everyone was when they thought champion skaters Tessa Virtue and Scott Moir were a romantic couple! Now that everyone knew Eric was gay, would judges wish he had a romance with Meagan?

For Meagan, Eric's sexuality was never an issue. She knew he was gay all along and always supported him. As best friends, they agreed that romance wouldn't be part of their performances. They had to win with a strong human connection and the best possible skate. It was a gamble, but Eric was on a mission. And he and Meagan succeeded!

At the 2018 PyeongChang Olympics, Eric made history. He and Meagan Duhamel won a gold medal in the team skating event. And they won the bronze medal in pairs skating! They waved to fans from the top of the podium. Eric was the first openly gay athlete to win an Olympic gold medal. It was a dream come true for the pair.

Eric helped make progress, but his job isn't done yet.

"There's a long road ahead of us," he said. "There's always room for improvement, but it's happening. There are more out figure skaters than ever before, and at the Olympics in general. The world is more accepting and more athletes are feeling comfortable coming out. It's something I can sense and feel from Olympics to Olympics."

He is right. Twenty-three athletes in the 2012 Summer Olympics were openly gay. By the 2016 Summer Olympics, 64 athletes were openly gay, lesbian or bisexual. The Winter Olympics also saw improvement. Seven openly gay women competed in the 2014 Winter Games in Sochi, Russia, despite that country's anti-LGBTQ+ laws. The number of gay athletes increased to 16 (12 women and 4 men) in the 2018 Winter Olympics. It marked the first time in Winter Olympic history that openly gay men competed.

PRIDE HOUSE

Pride House is a safe space for LGBTQ+ athletes — a place where everyone is welcome. It shows what the Olympic spirit is all about. The first Pride House was located at the 2010 Vancouver Olympics and Paralympics. Pride House was banned at the 2014 Games in Sochi, Russia, as part of that country's laws against LGBTQ+ people. In 2018, Eric Radford was one of the athletes — a group that also included Mark Tewksbury — who helped make Pride House possible again at the PyeongChang Games. That year, Pride House was part of Canada's space in the Olympic Village and Radford was there to welcome guests to the facility. Pride House inspired everyone at the Games, and made a big difference for LGBTQ+ athletes.

Eric is an ambassador for the Canadian Olympic Committee's #OneTeam initiative that fights to end homophobia in sports.

Eric retired from professional skating in 2018. He plays piano and writes music. He is now focusing on his music career, and on coaching and choreographing programs for other skaters. And he still supports LGBTQ+ athletes as an ambassador for the #OneTeam program.

"I've made a big difference by sharing my story — the internal struggle, external struggle, and everything I had to overcome," he said. "I worked hard and achieved my goals. If I can do it, it's possible for everyone else, too."

Eric's goal for the future is simple. "My hope is [that] eventually [being gay] won't matter for anyone — that questions about an athlete's sexuality won't be big news, and athletes will feel comfortable talking about their significant other, whether it's a boy or a girl," he said. "Athletes should be judged by their performance on the field of play, not for whom they love."

FIVE FACTS ABOUT ERIC RADFORD

- His first figure skates were white skates that his dad painted black.
- He's passionate about playing the piano and composing. He composed the music that Patrick Chan used for his free skate in the 2016–17 season, and he has his Grade 9 Royal Conservatory of Music certificate.
- He likes playing video games!
- One thousand people call Eric's hometown of Balmertown home. The town has one arena and a street named in Eric Radford's honour!
- While visiting the Wailing Wall in Jerusalem, he wrote his wish, "Win the World Championship," on a piece of paper and stuffed it between the cracks in the wall. That wish came true. Twice.

BETTY BAXTER
born July 8, 1952, in Brooks, Alberta

CAREER HIGHLIGHTS

- Captain, Canadian Olympic volleyball team, 1976

- Named head coach, Canadian national volleyball team, 1979

- Board member of the 1990 Gay Games in Vancouver

- Co-founded the Canadian Association for the Advancement of Women in Sport (now called Canadian Women & Sport) and the National Coaching School for Women.

- Ran as a New Democratic Party candidate in Vancouver Centre in 1993 federal election

- Elected school trustee in 2011

5
BAXTER AND LYE
Two Coaches, Two Different Experiences

There was a time when Betty Baxter felt like the only lesbian in the world.

It was 1970 and Betty was in her first year of university, where she played volleyball. She was a tall, strong girl from rural Alberta. She had always worn pants instead of skirts, been aggressive and powerful on the court and kept her hair cut short. She knew she was different from the women she saw in magazines.

But it wasn't until her first year of university that she realized she was gay. Betty didn't tell anybody. It was a time and a place where gays and lesbians didn't dare share their sexual orientation. "I was afraid that if anyone found out I was a lesbian, I would be kicked off the team and out of university housing," Betty explained. "Some of my teammates might have shunned me and called me a freak. Coaches didn't want anyone on the team who would cause problems socially. My objective was to play well, to make the first string, to win. The consequences were terrifyingly real."

Betty was unable to talk openly about being gay, to have a same-sex relationship or even connect with other lesbians. She kept her sexual identity a secret. At one point, she knew that two of her teammates were lesbians. All three were forced to have an underground social life.

They had secret talks or went for walks. "We were all under a lot of stress," Betty said.

It's easy to understand why. Every athlete on her team faced pressure to perform well. They had to earn a spot on the team, season after season. Being a lesbian threatened an athlete's chances of making the team. "Picking a team is subjective. The first five or six athletes are easy to choose," Betty explained. "If you're in the bottom three or four, or there's one spot left — if you're the LGB kid, you won't make the team. It's a judgment call."

Betty made it her mission to be the best at her sport. She couldn't afford not to be. "As an athlete, I had to be in the top."

Her mission was a success. She was on the Canadian women's volleyball team that competed in the 1976 Summer Olympics.

After the Olympics, Betty became a volleyball coach at the University of Ottawa. She was such a good coach that she won Coach of the Year for the Canadian Interuniversity Athletics Union. By 1979, she was hired as the head coach of Canada's women's volleyball team.

YOU CAN PLAY

You Can Play (YCP) is a non-profit organization dedicated to ending homophobia in sports.

It was founded in 2012 by Brian Kitts, Glenn Witman, former NHL general manager Brian Burke and Burke's son, NHL executive Patrick Burke. You Can Play was started in memory of hockey player Brendan Burke (Brian's son and Patrick's brother), who came out in 2009. Brendan had left the sport he loved because it was too homophobic. When he came out, he gave a face to the issue and made Canadians take a hard look at homophobia in sport. Tragically, Brendan died in a car accident a few months later, but his legacy lives on through You Can Play. Partners of You Can Play include the National Hockey League (NHL), the National Football League (NFL), the Canadian Football League (CFL), Major League Soccer (MLS) and many other sports leagues. It also works with Egale Canada Human Rights Trust and the Canadian Olympic Committee to make sports safe and inclusive for everyone. You Can Play offers training and education, and encourages athletes to march in Pride parades and to use their influence to create change.

"The dial is shifting, but the fact we're still talking about it . . . is an issue."

As a leader, Betty knew it was even more important to keep her sexuality a secret. "You were expected to be more of a [role] model. Even some of my allies feared that parents wouldn't send their young athletes to a program led by a lesbian."

But there were rumours. On January 17, 1982, Betty was fired from her head coaching job for no given reason. By then, even her allies — people who believed in her as a coach — agreed it would be better for the program if Betty wasn't part of it.

She left sports altogether. "It was profoundly hurtful," Betty said. "The sports system was so deeply corrupt. It was mind-blowing there wasn't a place I could be myself."

Betty's firing was a disgrace, and is known as a crucial moment in gay sports history. Things had to change. These days, Betty believes schools are doing a good job of teaching acceptance, not just tolerance. She is also excited about You Can Play, which she thinks has made more progress in sports in a few years than she'd seen in the 40 years before it was founded. She is also happy to see initiatives such as Canada's Pride House.

"Kids are seeing more openly gay role models. Canadian universities and the major sports leagues are supporting You Can Play," said Betty. "The dial is shifting, but the fact we're still talking about it — the fact these things are still needed — is an issue."

Betty is an activist, and promoting the idea that sport is for everyone — including coaches — is a big part of her goal. "It's not anywhere near half over," she said. "It's just the beginning."

After being forced out of coaching, Betty Baxter entered politics and served as a school trustee in British Columbia.

After Betty Baxter was fired from her coaching job, she helped establish the Canadian Association for the Advancement of Women and Sport (now called Canadian Women & Sport). The association was founded in 1981 in response to negative media coverage of women in sports and because of the barriers to women participating in sports. Back then, it was hard for women even to book a field or rink or to find a coach. Betty also founded the National Coaching School for Women. In 1990, she was on the board of the Gay Games in Vancouver, a global sporting and cultural event that promotes the acceptance of sexual diversity. Eventually, Betty moved into politics. In 1993, she became the first openly lesbian candidate to run for national office. Although she lost that election, she remained involved in politics, serving two terms as a school trustee in British Columbia.

JOEY LYE
born May 4, 1987, in
Toronto, Ontario

CAREER HIGHLIGHTS

- World Baseball Softball Confederation (WBSC) World Championship, 2010: bronze; 2012: 4th; 2014: 4th; 2016: bronze; 2018: bronze

- Pan American Games, 2011: silver; 2015: gold; 2019: silver

- WBSC Americas Qualifier, 2013: silver; 2017: bronze

- Member, Team Canada, women's softball, 2020

- Head coach, Bucknell softball team

Over time, things have changed for women's team sports. Just ask Olympic softball player Joey Lye. She grew up in Toronto and started playing softball and hockey at age seven. She loved being part of a team, chasing her goals and making progress in a sport. It gave her life focus and a chance to compete. But it was her hard work that helped her excel.

"I was always told I was too small to play at the levels I wanted to, and have never been a flashy player in either game," Joey admitted. But that just made her more determined. "I set out every day to prove that I could do it — whatever the 'it' was."

The idea that she'd never be good enough pushed Joey to be the hardest worker and helped her achieve her goals. And she set her goals very high. When she was in grade school, she wrote her autobiography. It was called *Future Olympian*.

As Joey grew up, she didn't know she was gay. She even had boyfriends. But it bothered her that when a few of her teammates came out, people weren't very welcoming and supportive of them. After college, Joey realized she was a lesbian. She was afraid to tell her parents in case they were disappointed. Soon, Joey felt like two people: her real self and the person her family thought she was. Living a lie was draining. Joey finally came out to her parents when she was 28. She wanted to be her full self and share the ups and downs of her relationships with her family.

It was terrifying for her. "My mom was shocked at first," she said. "It was a lot for her to swallow." Then, two months later, Joey called with more big news: she was getting married. This time, it was the fact that Joey was keeping a secret that her mother reacted to. "My mom was more upset that she wasn't in the know and fully involved in my life. She wasn't upset that I was gay."

Joey is proud that her parents came to the wedding. "My parents love my wife. I'm so happy with how everything has played out."

Now that she is free to be herself, Joey is happier and more positive than ever. She is especially happy to be on Canada's national softball team and an Olympic athlete. "I can train without so many unknowns. I don't have a cloud looming over me. There's nothing like being able to be who you are and feel loved for that."

Today, Joey feels completely accepted on the softball team. It wasn't always like that in women's sports. Thankfully, attitudes have changed. "When I started playing at high levels, our culture was in a different place," she said. "The team wasn't unsupportive and out players

"I think that having me as an openly gay coach makes things as normal as possible for them."

Joey high-fives teammates on the Canadian Wild National Pro Fastpitch team during the pregame lineup.

weren't treated any differently, but the coaching staff were shocked at first to understand female athletes wanted to talk about their personal lives."

It took a few years to adjust, but now the softball coaches are more open, too. The staff ask their athletes about their girlfriends and wives, and women talk about their orientation from the start. "We all treat each other as individuals, regardless of orientation," Joey said. "We care about each other. It's a supportive, open, and loving environment."

In addition to playing softball for Team Canada, Joey is also a softball coach at Pennsylvania's Bucknell University. As a university coach, she has the chance to do what Betty Baxter couldn't when she was coaching: be publicly out and a role model, and create a welcoming environment for every athlete on the team.

Playing softball for Team Canada and as head coach of a university team in the US, Joey's openness inspires her teammates and players.

"I'm so happy for younger generations coming out," Joey said. "The environment is so different now. A couple of athletes spoke to me when they were trying to figure out who they were. It's comforting to know they felt safe speaking to their coaches and teammates. I think that having me as an openly gay coach makes things as normal as possible for them."

Joey encourages her athletes to be open. She even led a vulnerability session where each athlete talked about the challenges in their life. "I talked about coming out to my mom and why that was hard for me."

Women playing and coaching sports at university and Olympic levels are feeling safer and more supported. But Joey knows that men on campus don't feel the same way. "I'm hearing that a lot of male athletes are closeted, that they don't have the same openness with their team, and that there is a lot of pressure to be macho and 'manly.' Our counselling centre gets a lot of athletes coming in because they don't feel comfortable in the athletic space, in fraternities, or at school in general."

Today, many universities are having discussions about how to make campuses more open and accepting. Coaches are being trained so they can better help LGBTQ+ students who are struggling.

SUPPORTING GAY COACHES

According to research by Jennifer Birch-Jones of Canadian Women & Sport (CWS), there are still few openly gay coaches. Many gay coaches worry that athletes won't want to play for them or that people think they will openly promote "a gay lifestyle." "Coaches believe that coming out will cause more problems and pose more risks than concealing their sexual orientation." As part of their inclusion in sport initiative, the CWS created a guide called *Leading the Way: Working with LGBTQ Athletes and Coaches* to help make sure sports is a safe and respectful place for everyone, including LGBTQ+ players and coaches.

CINDY OUELLET

born December 8, 1988, in Rivière-du-Loup, Quebec

CAREER HIGHLIGHTS

- Wheelchair Basketball Canada Junior Athlete of the Year, 2007

- All-Star, Canadian Wheelchair Basketball League (CWBL) Women's National Championship, 2010, 2012, 2014, 2015, 2017, 2018

- MVP, CWBL Women's National Championship, 2011, 2013, 2016

- All-Star, 2011 Women's U25 World Championship

- Wheelchair Basketball Canada Female Athlete of the Year, 2012, 2016, 2017, 2018

- Received Queen Elizabeth II Diamond Jubilee Medal, 2013

- Led all players in assists at the 2014 Women's World Championship

- One of few athletes to compete in the Winter and Summer Paralympic Games: 2009, 2012 and 2016 Summer Games; 2018 Winter Games (para Nordic skiing)

6
CINDY OUELLET
Female, Gay and Paralympian

rowing up in Rivière-du-Loup, Quebec, Cindy Ouellet was a tomboy who loved playing sports. She was an elite skier and soccer player who also had a passion for music.
Cindy's sexual orientation wasn't something she understood or thought about as a kid. But
her parents always told their only child that they would accept her however she was. "It was
like my parents knew all along," Cindy said. At the time, all Cindy wanted to do was play
sports.

But then the unthinkable happened. When she was 11 years old, Cindy was hit from
behind while playing football. She broke her hip. But tests showed it wasn't just an ordinary
break. Doctors found a tumour in her left hip. Cindy was diagnosed with Ewing's sarcoma,
or bone cancer, at age 12.

"There was only a 5 per cent chance I'd recover," she said. She had to do everything she could
to stay alive. Over the next several years, Cindy underwent 28 chemotherapy treatments and had
surgery to remove her left pelvis and femur (thighbone). The treatments damaged the nerves
going into her legs, and she was left with no feeling or movement in her left leg. Her leg was

After Cindy Ouellet was hit during a football game when she was 12, doctors found a tumour in her left hip.

replaced with the technology that was available at the time. But it was the wheelchair that Cindy took to. Though she can walk with crutches today, Cindy has preferred her wheelchair ever since. "It makes it easier to get around ... and faster," she said in an interview.

Cindy returned to high school when she was 15. It was a difficult year. Other kids bullied her for being new, and for being bald, as she had lost her hair during the cancer treatments. It was during that year she also realized she was gay. Coming out to her parents was scary, but they had supported her through everything. She knew she had to tell them. Their reaction was a relief to Cindy. "Everyone was supportive," she said. "My parents were positive. They said it didn't matter or change who I was. They didn't see me as a different person."

Her parents' backing gave Cindy the strength to focus on getting back to what she loved most: sports. Her father had started a business building adaptive sports equipment for people with disabilities — people like his daughter. Cindy got into para-swimming and para-track at age 16. At around the same time, in 2005, her physiotherapist suggested she play basketball. It was a sport she had never played before she got cancer. But Cindy fell in love with it right away.

Cindy wouldn't change her success in wheelchair basketball for the use of her legs. She once told the *Toronto Star* she's happy the way she is.

WHEELCHAIR BASKETBALL

Wheelchair basketball is a rough, fast-paced, competitive sport. Each team has five players and seven substitutes. Some rules are similar to the standing game. For instance, the game is played on a regulation-sized, marked hardwood court. The court dimensions, height of the net and distance to the foul and three-point lines are the same. Scoring is the same, too: a goal from the free-throw line is one point; two points from the field goal line; and three points from the three-point line. The shot clock is set to 24 seconds before the ball goes to the other team. There are four periods of 10 minutes. Overtime is five minutes long. Dribbling is a bit different: players can push or touch their wheels two times before they must dribble the ball. Travelling will be called if the player takes more than two pushes without dribbling. Athletes must stay seated in their chair and cannot use their legs. If a player falls out of the chair, a referee can stop the play if there is a risk of injury; otherwise, the game continues.

Cindy trained hard. She had to learn how to shoot a basketball, and also how to manoeuvre around the court in a wheelchair. In time, she became fast and efficient at the game. It was a physical and demanding sport, but Cindy never gave up, even when she got hurt. "It is supposed to be a no contact sport, but it really isn't," she told the *Toronto Star*. "It's like stand-up basketball, but I think it's more physical because of the chair contact."

She has been injured many times. "I got a couple of dislocated shoulders, sprained fingers, broken fingers, a broken hand." She has also had a double concussion and a skull fracture. "It's pretty rough."

But Cindy persisted, and thrived. By 2007, she had won a gold medal for Quebec at the Canada Games and made the senior women's national team. By age 18, she received a full scholarship to the University of Alabama, where she studied exercise science and played for their women's wheelchair basketball team. While earning both her undergraduate and graduate degrees there, Cindy practised three times a day. This helped her get a place on Team Canada. Cindy represented Canada at the 2008 Paralympic Games in Beijing,

"I want to keep proving that I'm no different than any other athlete."

the London 2012 Paralympic Games and the Rio 2016 Paralympics. In 2011, she made Canada's first-ever Women's U25 National Team. She was named to the all-star team and finished fourth in overall tournament scoring. Averaging 20 points per game at the University of Alabama, Cindy helped her school win a national championship title in 2011 and 2015.

Basketball is not Cindy's only sport. In 2018, she represented Canada in para Nordic skiing at the Paralympics in PyeongChang, making her one of the few athletes in the world to compete at both the Summer and Winter Paralympic Games.

What Cindy has found while competing in both basketball and skiing is that Paralympic sport is a very open and welcoming community when it comes to sexual orientation. "There are a lot of inequalities in sport — I was already in a chair, I'm a girl, and I'm gay," she said. "But I've only ever had a positive experience in sport."

WHAT IS INTERSECTIONALITY?

Sadly, people tend to face discrimination for a number of different reasons — ignorance, prejudice, sexism, racism and homophobia. *Intersectionality* describes how a person's identities overlap in a way that makes them more likely to be discriminated against by some people in society. Factors include race, gender, class, sexual orientation, ethnicity and disability. For instance, Cindy Ouellet learned to thrive despite prejudices against various intersecting factors: being gay, being a woman and being in a wheelchair.

Cindy also competes in cross-fit and works hard to maintain her strength.

By the time Cindy made the national basketball team, other openly LGBTQ+ athletes had already paved the way. She found that her teammates and coaches and the national association were very understanding. The only time she might have felt otherwise was when she was a student in Alabama. "I had to be mindful about being openly gay there," she said. "In Canada, I don't feel judged. I'm open and I am who I am."

Cindy wants to be seen as an athlete, not as a gay athlete. "I want to keep proving that I'm no different than any other athlete."

Yet she is so much more than a typical athlete. She is active as an ambassador for several organizations that help kids in areas involving sport, bullying, cancer, disabilities and sexuality. Her goal is simple: "I want to help provide a safe environment for everyone, so that men and women can be free in their own environment."

In addition to all her outreach activities, Cindy also travels around the world playing basketball for Team Canada. But like Eric Radford, sport is not the only thing Cindy plays. She is very musical, and plays piano, guitar, drums and even the ukulele. In addition, Cindy speaks to different groups to share her story and her message. When she's home in Quebec, she works with her father making adaptive equipment for people with disabilities. And she studies, being on a full scholarship to earn her Ph.D. in Biomedical Engineering through the University of Southern California. Once she has her degree, Cindy plans to continue creating equipment for people with disabilities. And she has no intention to quit playing competitive sports anytime soon.

A BRIEF HISTORY OF THE PARALYMPIC GAMES

In 1948, the Paralympics began as a wheelchair competition for injured war veterans in England. It was held the same day as the opening ceremony of the London Olympic Games.

The first of what would eventually be called the Paralympic Games was held in 1960 in Rome. Four hundred athletes from 23 countries competed.

Canada participated in its first Paralympic Games in Tel Aviv, Israel, in 1968. Canada sent 25 athletes and won 19 medals.

Since those early days, the Paralympic Games has grown to become one of the largest world-wide sporting events. Athletes compete in several categories that are broken into classifications that vary from sport to sport.

The London 2012 Games broke all records: 4,200 athletes from 160 countries competed in 20 sports.

Since the 1988 Summer Games in Seoul, South Korea, both the Winter and Summer Paralympic Games have been held after the Olympic Games have finished, instead of at the same time.

Other major Olympic competitions include the Special Olympics World Games for athletes with intellectual disabilities, and the Deaflympics for athletes who are hearing impaired.

ANGELA JAMES
born December 22, 1964, in Toronto, Ontario

CAREER HIGHLIGHTS

- Member of Canada's national team at the first World Women's Hockey Championship; set a record, scoring 11 goals in five games, 1990

- Helped Canada's national team win gold in 1990, 1992, 1994 and 1997

- Awards: Toronto's Women in Sport Enhancement (1992); Hockey Canada's Female Hockey Breakthrough (2005)

- Inductee: Black Hockey and Sports Hall of Fame (2006); Canada's Sports Hall of Fame (2009); Ice Hockey Federation Hockey Hall of Fame (2008); first woman inducted into the Hockey Hall of Fame (2010); Ontario Sport Hall of Fame (2019)

7
JAMES AND OUELLETTE
Changing Times in Women's Hockey

Growing up in the 1960s and '70s, Angela James had it tough. She was mixed race, gay and raised by a single mom in a poor neighbourhood in Toronto. While other kids got into trouble, Angela focused on the sport she loved most: hockey.

There weren't any girls' hockey leagues at that time, so when Angela was seven, her mom signed her up to play with the boys. The league didn't want girls playing, but Angela's mother didn't think that was right. She threatened to call a lawyer if they didn't let her daughter play. By the next year, Angela was so good she was moved up several levels. She played with 11- and 12-year-old boys when she was just eight! After that, the league told her she had to play with girls. The all-girls league wasn't close by, so Angela had to take a long bus ride with all her equipment to get to her games. But she was such a good player that her family made a lot of sacrifices so she could keep playing.

It was worth it. In 1980, Angela turned 16. She joined the Central Ontario Women's Hockey League and played there until 1998, when her team became part of the National Women's Hockey League. Angela was considered the fiercest female hockey player in Canada. She was even called the Wayne Gretzky of women's hockey. She usually played centre forward, but she was also good at defence. She had a hard and fast shot, scored a lot of goals and was

"I don't discuss my personal life. I'd rather know the score of last night's game."

known for her aggressive style of play. One time, her team had no goalie, so James put on the goalie equipment — and recorded a shutout!

Angela played on Canada's national team at the first World Women's Hockey Championship in 1990. She set a record, scoring 11 goals in five games, and helped the team win the gold medal. Then, in 1992, 1994 and 1997, she did it again.

In 1998, for the first time ever, women's hockey was going to be an Olympic event. But something shocking happened: Angela was cut from the team. How could this happen? Angela was the best player in Canada!

Angela asked the organizers to reconsider. But she was gay and people were saying she was the coach's girlfriend. Her appeal was turned down. Angela wouldn't be on the first Canadian women's hockey team to compete at the Olympics. "Homophobia ruined my appeal, because something got all blown up and the direction went there, instead of towards my appeal," Angela said in an interview.

Angela was proud of who she was, but she was a private person. She didn't want to be an advocate or spokesperson. "[People] know what I am, who I'm with, and about my family — I'm open," she said. "But I don't discuss my personal life. I'd rather know the score of last night's game."

It took a long time, but Angela has been recognized for being an amazing hockey player. In 2010, she was the first woman — and the first openly out lesbian — to be inducted into the Hockey Hall of Fame. At the induction ceremony, Angela thanked her wife in her speech and didn't care what anyone thought. "I am who I am," she said afterward. "I'm proud of my partner and family, and the more people that can say that, the better. If people have an issue with this, then too bad. Today, male coaches and [general managers] have gay sons and daughters, and when they are very open and supportive, it helps. [But] it doesn't matter if I'm gay, straight, black, yellow, pink, polka-dot, or blue, I'm still the same person every day. I respect people for who they are."

Sometimes, women have shied away from playing hockey, traditionally considered a men's sport, for fear they'll be called a lesbian, whether they are or not. Lesbians have felt safer hiding their sexual identity or not playing hockey at all. Today, things are different. There are more women's hockey leagues than ever before, and registration in girls' hockey continues to increase each year. Today, all Canadians love cheering for the Canadian women's hockey team in the Olympics.

Women's and men's hockey are the same when it comes to the rules, the intensity and the excitement. But in the dressing room, it's another story. Today, women's hockey stands out for creating a more accepting culture than many other team sports.

Charline Labonté — Comfortable in the Net

"I am fortunate to have been a part of the Canadian women's national hockey team for 12 years, and I never felt I couldn't be free," said Charline Labonté. During her playing career, she won three Olympic gold medals, two World Championships and five World silver medals as the goalie for Team Canada. "Just like everywhere else, our team had gays and straights, just like we had brunettes and redheads. Everyone on my team has known I [was] gay since I can remember, and I never felt degraded for it. On the contrary, my sport and my team are the two environments where I feel most comfortable." Charline came out in 2014. Though nobody wanted to talk about their sexuality when Angela James played, it's different now. "Just a few years ago this topic was never a part of the conversations in the locker room," Charline said. "We talk and laugh about it like everything else."

CAROLINE OUELLETTE
born May 25, 1979, in Montreal, Quebec

CAREER HIGHLIGHTS

- Four-time Olympic gold-medal champion: Salt Lake City 2002, Turin 2006, Vancouver 2010, Sochi 2014

- Six-time World Champion: 1999–2001, 2004, 2007, 2012

- Six-time World silver medallist: 2005, 2008–09, 2011, 2013, 2015

- Graduate, Criminology and Women's Studies, University of Minnesota Duluth (2005)

- Event founder, Girls' Hockey Celebration

- Named Officer of the Order of Canada, 2019

Caroline Ouellette has noticed a change, even since she started playing at the elite level. She joined Canada's national hockey team in 1999 and won four Olympic gold medals between 2002 and 2014. Caroline says that, at the start of her Olympic career, athletes didn't talk about whether they loved men or women. "But it changed quickly. We became really accepting."

Proud to Play

How did that change happen?

"As more and more athletes said they were in a relationship with another woman, it made it more normal and acceptable," Caroline said. "Everyone realized they had friends who were gay, and it [being gay] didn't change the way we played or carried ourselves in training. The more present and common it was, the quicker it became accepted. It's about people having the courage to say who they are and live the way they want to live."

Caroline helped make the topic of gay families more common when she and her partner, American national hockey player Julie Chu, announced the arrival of their baby. Liv was born in 2017. In sharing the happy news, talking about their pregnancy and motherhood, Caroline helped normalize a subject that nobody ever used to talk about. "If you look back at the first women who had babies together, it wasn't something that was celebrated," Caroline said. "We were very overwhelmed with how supportive everyone was when we decided to speak about having Liv together. We're happy that society is accepting of it."

Fans and media were delighted with the couple's baby news. They asked if Liv would wear an American or Canadian hockey jersey. They wondered how soon the baby would learn to skate. It was a celebration of life, a happy moment that brought together hockey fans on both sides of the border.

She was also touched at a recent practice when a coach gave a pep talk to his team before their final match. "He told the girls they would have to be very disciplined and make sure

"It's about people having the courage to say who they are and live the way they want to live."

their boyfriend or girlfriend was supportive," she related. "He was coaching girls who were 15 or 16 years old, and was [being] inclusive. He knows the athletes might have boyfriends or girlfriends, and he made it a totally normal thing. We're seeing it more and more."

Women's sport still has a long way to go before it's equal to men's sports in many ways. Right now, the salaries of female players are lower, and so is the amount of exposure they get on TV. But in some ways, it's ahead of the pack. It's no wonder the Canadian Women's Hockey League (CWHL) was the first professional sports league to partner with You Can Play, in December 2012. The two organizations worked together to make the sport more inclusive for fans, players and coaches.

Caroline Ouellette (left) and her partner, American national hockey player Julie Chu, with their baby, Liv.

At the start of Caroline's Olympic career, athletes didn't talk about their sexual orientation.

Caroline hopes she can continue to make a difference as a role model for other girls. In addition to being moms, Caroline and Julie coach women's hockey, and Caroline runs a hockey school for girls and adults. She said their goal is to promote the sport and help girls become great athletes and people. And it seems they are achieving that goal. "I see little girls talking about Julie as my wife, and it's totally normal the way they say it," Caroline said.

CHRIS VOTH

born September 27, 1990,
in Winnipeg, Manitoba

CAREER HIGHLIGHTS

- The Netherlands: Dutch Cup 2015/2016, Super Cup 2015, North Dutch Cup 2015, Eredivisie (Netherlands League) 2015/2016 champion

- FISU Games, Shenzhen, China, 2011: 4th place; Kazan, Russia, 2013: 5th place

- CIS bronze 2011/2012 in Kingston, Ontario

- Former Ontario Hockey League and professional hockey player

- Played professionally in the United States and Europe

- First professional hockey player to come out as gay

- Advocate for the LGBTQ+ community and speaks at conferences, corporations, events and schools

- His story has been shared in newspapers and blogs across North America

- Three-time MHSAA volleyball champion: indoor, 2006 and 2007; beach, 2008

- Western Canada Summer Games champion 2007, Sherwood Park, Alberta

8
CHRIS VOTH
Canada's 1st Openly Gay Male Athlete on a National Team

Chris Voth plays volleyball, and he knows what it's like to come out. He is one of the few openly gay men on a national sports team. A Canadian volleyball star, Chris came out in an article in the *Winnipeg Free Press* in January 2014 while at the peak of his career. His announcement made him the first openly gay athlete to play on a national men's team. Coming out wasn't easy for Chris. At age 23, he worried about ruining his relationship with his parents, who had conservative beliefs. He also didn't know how his teammates would react. "Volleyball isn't a contact sport, and it's not 'macho,' but it's still tough to come out," Chris said. "You train a lot; your teammates are your friends. And unlike in other sports, you really rely on your team. You have to pass to each other. You have to trust each other."

Luckily, the volleyball culture is team-oriented, and Chris found an accepting community. His teammates congratulated him for his courage. And since volleyball is lower-profile than other professional sports, Chris didn't have to think about losing endorsements or having a tough-guy image.

But there was still one unknown. Chris had graduated from university and wanted a contract on a professional volleyball team in Europe. Would his sexuality affect his career overseas? Sadly, it did. In 2017, Chris lost a contract because he was gay.

When Chris Voth came out in 2014, he became the first openly gay athlete to play on a national men's team.

That's when he decided to talk to the media about what had happened. Canadians were in shock. How could this volleyball star be passed over for a sports contract because of his sexual orientation? Chris's story was one of the most shared articles online at the time. Readers wanted to hear his message. The issue also exposed a major problem in men's team sports.

"There's still not a lot of gay athletes on team sports who have come out," Chris observed. "We're progressing, and good work is being done across Canada to make sports more inclusive. It's really positive. But how far have we come at the highest levels?" He believes we have not come far enough, as there are not many out athletes on the national teams.

Chris wrote an article for the *Huffington Post* called "We Need More Gay Male Pro Team Sport Athletes to Come Out." In it, he pointed to statistics. In three Summer Olympics (2008, 2012 and 2016), 60 to 65 per cent of the out gay women competing belonged to a team sport. "On the men's side, none of the openly gay athletes were [in] a team sport," he wrote.

Chris believes he knows why. "Sport has always been a test of masculinity, going back from the beginning where you would compete to see who was the strongest or fastest," he wrote. "Today, sport has evolved into having a large psychological component with the necessity of evolved techniques, tactics and team play. Our perception of sport hasn't changed though . . . Gay men are still stereotyped to be more feminine than their straight counterparts, as opposed to gay women who are stereotyped to be more masculine [and therefore stronger competitors]."

"It is possible to be out and still succeed in sport."

Chris Voth

"I hope that by being a voice for gay athletes that I can be a part of the solution."

Chris worries about these stereotypes. He doesn't want people to think that gay men don't enjoy sports the way straight men do, that gay men are weaker athletes and that gay men have to worry about their teammates' feelings. By coming out during his career — and encouraging other gay team-based athletes to join him — Chris tried to prove those stereotypes wrong.

"I hope that by being a voice for gay athletes that I can be a part of the solution," Chris told OneVolleyball.org. "I'm hoping to inspire others to come out and to show that it is possible to be out and still succeed in sport."

Chris is involved in Out There Winnipeg, a safe and welcoming sports and recreation league. He and his Finnish volleyball team were the first professional volleyball team in the world to walk in a Pride parade. The parade took place days after Finland legalized same-sex marriage. "It was amazing to have the support of my club and teammates, and it sent a strong message to the rest of the sport community," Chris said.

Chris coaches volleyball at the university level and is president of Out There Winnipeg, a welcoming recreational sports league.

Chris Voth

JESSICA PLATT
born May 8, 1989, in Sarnia, Ontario

CAREER HIGHLIGHTS

- 2016: Drafted into the Canadian Women's Hockey League, 61st overall pick

- 2017–18: played full-time for the Toronto Furies

- Recognized as one of Canada's Women of Influence's "Top 25 Women of Influence 2018."

- Advocate, transgender rights

9

JESSICA PLATT
The 1st Openly Transgender Athlete in Canadian Professional Hockey

The athlete we now know as Jessica Platt was once a shy boy. He loved hockey, but didn't have any friends on his hockey team. He was always the first player dressed and ready to leave the change room.

Nobody could tell by looking at him, but on the inside, something was different. He didn't feel comfortable with the way the boys behaved in the dressing room. They would say mean things about gay people, girls and anyone else who was different. Sometimes, just to fit in, he would say mean things too, but mostly he stayed quiet. He was more at ease with girls and preferred playing with dolls.

During puberty, when everyone's bodies began changing, he didn't like the changes happening in his body. It felt unfair, but he didn't understand why. He kept himself as busy as possible so he wouldn't have time to think about how confused and depressed he felt. He played hockey and joined the school band. He worked at Tim Hortons and at his family's flower shop in Sarnia, Ontario. Yet the more different and confused he felt, the more time he spent alone on his computer. "When I was at home, I didn't really want to be around people," says Jessica now. "I started realizing I was different. I was scared of how my family would react. I didn't know if they would reject me or still love me. I started isolating myself

As a child, Jessica Platt loved playing hockey. On the ice, she could be herself.

from them, trying to Google how I was feeling and what it meant."

He learned about being transgender on the internet. It's how he realized he was a she. It was a big moment — a moment in which he started thinking of himself as a young woman.

Jessica was from a city that didn't have much diversity. She didn't know anything about LGBTQ+ people. There was nobody to talk to about the fact she was born physically a boy, but knew she was a girl. It was a low point in her life. She took a few years off after high school to work. She drank alcohol to numb the pain and to get through her days. Eventually, she saw a counsellor who encouraged her to go back to school. She also found videos on YouTube showing people transitioning into the gender they needed to be.

"I'd watch transition compilation videos and could see how happy they [the transgender people] were getting as pictures progressed," said Jessica. She was talking about videos where someone born in a male body would change into their female body over time. "It helped me a lot. It showed me what I could potentially do — that I could be happy; that

"I wanted people to look to me and see someone happy, loving life, and loving themselves."

there were options."

Eventually, Jessica packed up her things and went off to Wilfrid Laurier University. Away from her small town, she felt free to be herself. A woman. She grew her hair long, put on makeup and wore tighter, more feminine clothing. Her roommates and friends encouraged her to be herself. In her second year, she began using the name Jessica. She was treated exactly how she wanted to be treated. "This made a huge difference for me," Jessica remembered. "It solidified who I was. I felt validated. Natural."

She was scared to take the next step, but now that she was feeling more like herself, Jessica knew it was time. She told her mom, siblings and then her dad. Afraid of disappointing her father, she told him by email. He was confused at first, so Jessica explained her decision to transition. "Once he understood, he was incredible," she said.

Jessica's father, Richard, told his daughter that nothing she could do would ever disappoint him. He was proud of her strength.

"It was pretty special for me," Jessica said. "I'm thankful for the positive support I got from my family."

She legally changed her name to Jessica and began transitioning to a woman. It wasn't easy getting the hormone replacement pills that would make her voice, her skin and her body more feminine. But all the appointments with doctors and psychiatrists were worth it. "I liked seeing a more feminine version of myself emerge . . . Changes happened very gradually, but it made me happy," she said.

Her mom even went to Montreal with her for gender confirming surgery. This is where a person's chest and/or private parts are surgically changed to align with the gender a person is becoming. It took Jessica months to recover, but finally she was ready to return to her active lifestyle. Her body was completely different — she was sixty pounds lighter than when she began her transition. Her body had become slower and less muscular during the process and because of the training she did pre- and post-surgery. But she began training hard once again. She went to the gym six days a week. She ran 10-kilometre races and duathlons.

While teaching kids how to skate and play hockey, Jessica remembered how much she

After gender confirming surgery, Jessica worked hard to regain her strength and stamina.

loved the sport. She signed up for a competitive hockey league. She loved it so much she wanted to play hockey at a higher level. She ran, biked, weight-trained and did whatever she could to get stronger and faster. Her goal was to register for the 2016 Canadian Women's Hockey League (CWHL) draft.

Jessica's determination and hard work paid off. She was drafted to the Toronto Furies in 2016 and added to the reserve roster. That meant she could play when they needed her, but she wasn't on the full-time team. She worked even harder. The next season she made the roster and played nearly every game.

In January 2018, at age 28, the once-shy athlete was ready to be the centre of attention. She decided to tell her story to the media. She didn't know how the CWHL or her teammates would react. But she knew that being a visible role model would help other

Jessica met her goal of playing on a women's pro hockey team when she made the roster of the Toronto Furies in 2017.

transgender kids feel better about themselves. She remembered being inspired by a Nike commercial featuring American transgender athlete Chris Mosier. She was also inspired by Canadian transgender hockey player Harrison Browne. Born female, Harrison Browne was the first openly transgender professional hockey player. He played for the National Women's Hockey League before retiring in 2018.

"I saw how people responded to them and the positive impact they had on others," Jessica remembered. "I thought back to when I was young and had nobody to look to. I had no idea that I could transition, be happy, and still follow my dreams. I wanted people to look to me and see someone happy, loving life, and loving themselves. I wanted to show people

Chris Mosier — Unlimited Courage

Chris Mosier is the first openly transgender person to play for a US National Team. He began his physical transition from a woman to a man in 2010. In 2015 he made Team USA's men's sprint duathlon for the 2016 World Championship. He was the first transgender athlete to star in a Nike ad, which aired during the 2016 Rio Olympics. Mosier is an advocate for trans inclusion in sport, founding TransAthlete.com and working for and with You Can Play to ensure LGBTQ+ athletes, coaches and fans feel safe and included in sports.

it's possible to be happy."

When Jessica made her announcement, she became the first openly transgender athlete in the CWHL. The league publicly congratulated her. Platt's team hugged her. She also received hundreds of messages of support on social media, including one from Harrison Browne. "You are saving lives," he tweeted.

While Harrison and Jessica have had positive experiences as transgender hockey players, it's often not the case for athletes who are transgender. In fact, this is a new and confusing area of sports where rules are being made and changed and made again. People are still arguing about who should be allowed to participate in men's and women's sports. Nobody can agree on what's fair.

Because of these debates, rules are different for each sport, in each country and depending on what level of sport is played. At most elite levels, like the Olympics, transgender men aren't seen to have a competitive advantage over other male competitors. People don't think they will be as fast or as strong as other men. At the Olympics, they are allowed to compete in men's sports without any restrictions.

But for transgender women, it's different. Some people don't think transgender women should be allowed to participate in women's sport at all. They think these athletes have an unfair advantage and will win. Some of the arguments are based on the fact that men typically have more testosterone than women. Testosterone is a hormone that can make athletes stronger and faster. There is no conclusive proof of how big a role testosterone plays in sports performance. However, a lot of people think that higher testosterone levels give athletes who are assigned the male sex at birth an unfair advantage, even after they transition.

In 2004, the International Olympic Committee (IOC) allowed transgender athletes to participate in the Olympic Games. There were three rules. First: athletes needed to have had "sex reassignment" or gender confirmation surgery. Second: athletes had to show they were legally the gender they said they were. Third: athletes had to have taken hormone therapy for two years before competing.

Things changed again in 2015. The IOC agreed that the rules they set 11 years before weren't fair. It wasn't right to make athletes have surgery to compete. In some countries, gender transition wasn't even legal. The new guidelines — in effect since the 2016 Rio Olympics — state that trans woman athletes have to state their gender and not change it for four years. They also have to have a testosterone level of less than 10 nanomoles/litre for at least one year before competition. No openly transgender athletes competed in the 2016 Olympics.

But there are even more complications. Some women are born intersex, which can cause their body to naturally produce more testosterone than most women. They are born with a body that falls outside of being male or female, affecting hormones and other sex characteristics. Athletes like Caster Semenya and Dutee Chand have both faced challenges from the IOC and sport governing bodies because of their higher levels of testosterone and queer identities.

THE TESTOSTERONE MYTH

It is widely believed that having more testosterone automatically makes athletes better in sports. Experts like Drs. Katrina Karkazis and Rebecca M. Jordan-Young say this is a myth. In a 2019 article in the *New York Times*, they wrote: "Labeling testosterone the male sex hormone suggests that it is restricted to men and is alien to women's bodies . . . women also produce and require testosterone as part of healthy functioning."

Their work shows that more testosterone doesn't automatically equal better athletic ability — it has many complex functions in the body. The researchers point to an analysis by the International Association of Athletics Federations that involved more than 1,100 women competing in track and field events. This study showed that women with lower testosterone did better than those with higher levels in 3 of 11 events. The myth that testosterone makes athletes better leads to discrimination against both female athletes with naturally higher levels of testosterone and transgender women. It also leads sporting bodies to create rules that aren't fair for everyone. Drs. Karkazis and Jordan-Young hope their work will help people rethink what they know about testosterone and fairness in sport.

Sports organizations are debating whether these women should be forced to take drugs to lower their testosterone to a certain level before they can compete. Instead of altering intersex bodies, many people are fighting to ensure that intersex people are included at the highest level of sport with the body they were born in.

In 2018, Canadian universities released a new policy for trans athletes. The rules state that transgender athletes can participate on varsity sports teams that match either the sex they are assigned at birth or the gender they are now. There is even a drug policy exemption so athletes who are transitioning can take the medicine they need and still compete. It took a long time and a lot of discussion to create these policies. People wanted university sports to include everyone.

Many athletes and organizations, including Harrison Browne, Jessica Platt and You Can Play (which both athletes work for) are using their voices and sharing their stories to make sure every athlete feels included. They want everyone to have the chance to be proud to play.

Rachel McKinnon — Sparking Controversy

In October 2018, Canadian transgender cyclist Rachel McKinnon won a gold medal at the UCI Masters Track Cycling World Championship in Los Angeles. Some people — including the athlete who placed third in the race — were angry. They said it was unfair that Rachel won. They said trans women shouldn't be allowed to participate in women's sports. Rachel received death threats, but she fought back. Rachel is a researcher, athlete and advocate and she could handle the debate. She said her hormone levels were in the right range to compete. She had followed the rules for transgender athletes. She had worked hard and won fairly. Rachel also pointed out that studies show high testosterone levels don't automatically make someone a better athlete. Her win sparked a big debate around the world. People are still arguing about the rights of transgender athletes and the rules around their participation in sports. The debate continues.

BROCK McGILLIS

born October 1, 1983, in Sudbury, Ontario

- Former Ontario Hockey League and professional hockey player

- Played professionally in the United States and Europe

- First professional hockey player to come out as gay

- Advocate for the LGBTQ+ community and speaks at conferences, corporations, events and schools

- His story has been shared in newspapers and blogs across North America

10
BROCK McGILLIS
The Big Four and "Locker Room" Culture

Brock McGillis narrowed his eyes and crouched in his net. Kitchener Rangers all-star Derek Roy skated toward him on a power play, coming in fast. McGillis kept his eyes on the puck. As the starting goalie for the Windsor Spitfires, McGillis was the team's last line of defence. Everyone was counting on him to make the save.

In that moment, McGillis would rather have been lying in bed than standing in net. His head was fuzzy. The night before, he had cried all night. He had had too much to drink. Again. The eighteen-year-old hadn't slept well in days.

McGillis is gay. Most days he hated himself for it. Hated who he pretended to be in the locker room after every game. Hated to hear words like *fag* come out of his own mouth. It's how some athletes trash talk players on other teams, so he did it too. All he wanted was to fit in. To be part of the group.

Roy charged toward the crease, then cut across the ice. He drew back his stick and took a shot. McGillis deflected the puck with his stick and pad. The puck bounced off an opposing player's chest, giving the Rangers a chance at the rebound.

McGillis dove across the net to stop the puck. In his scramble, his blocker fell off, leaving his right hand exposed. He landed on the ice. As the puck flew over his head, a teammate skated over McGillis's hand.

The Rangers scored.

McGillis looked down in shame. Crimson blood poured out onto the ice. That's when he realized that blood was shooting out of his hand. He could see right down to the bone. As he was rushed by ambulance to the hospital, McGillis knew this would be a season-ending injury.

He couldn't have been more relieved.

Fast forward a few years.

On April 19, 2016, Andrew Shaw of the Chicago Blackhawks yelled a homophobic slur at a referee during a National Hockey League playoff game. The league suspended him for one game, sent him to sensitivity training and fined him $5,000. A year later, it happened in Major League Baseball: Kevin Pillar, then centre-fielder for the Toronto Blue Jays, shouted a gay insult at a pitcher and was suspended for two games. The next day, the spotlight was back on the NHL. Anaheim Ducks captain Ryan Getzlaf also used homophobic language in a big game against the Nashville Predators. He was fined $10,000.

Brock McGillis had seen enough. As the only out former professional hockey player, he told the media that a $10,000 fine wasn't a serious enough consequence. He said that homophobia is a big problem in hockey — and not just in the NHL. It's a problem in minor hockey, too.

"I thought being gay was wrong," Brock told CBC News. "I thought it was bad. And that was all based off language I heard in locker rooms, language I heard on the ice. We have to program kids at Tyke [level], at Novice [level], at younger ages so they grow up thinking this [homophobia] is wrong — so the gay kid in the room feels safe."

Cheryl MacDonald is a sports psychologist, and studies homophobia in hockey. To find out how much of a problem homophobia is in the game, she interviewed more than 100 hockey players at all levels. She found that these athletes had been taught to behave in certain ways so they don't appear weak. They have learned over time to make jokes about gay people and brag about their sexual encounters with women.

Today, Brock talks about his experiences and works with hockey players to change the locker room culture.

Brock McGillis experienced this firsthand. "Hockey has always been very homophobic," he wrote when he came out in 2016. "I can't count the amount of times I heard phrases like 'That's gay' or 'What a homo' in the dressing room over the course of my hockey career. Words like *fag*, *p---y*, and *b---h* are part of the daily banter. Those words are used to belittle players, to weaken and feminize them, because hockey is hyper-masculine, meant for the manliest of men."

In 2019 there wasn't a single NHL player — retired or active — who was out.

But some pro athletes have come out while actively playing. The NBA's Jason Collins made headlines in 2013 when he announced he was gay. It made him the first active openly gay male athlete playing in a Big Four (Major League Baseball, the National Basketball Association, the National Football League and the National Hockey League) sports league. In a *Sports Illustrated* article, Collins wrote, "If I had my way, someone else would have already done this. Nobody has, which is why I'm raising my hand." He retired the following year after a 13-year career.

"One day, trust me, you will come out and it will feel liberating. You will persevere."

Robbie Rogers, a pro soccer player, came out in 2013, too, a day after retiring from European soccer. That year, he joined the Los Angeles Galaxy and became the only openly gay professional soccer player in North America. He retired in 2017.

Then there is Michael Sam. He was already open to teammates at the University of Missouri about being gay. He came out publicly before the 2014 NFL draft and was taken by the St. Louis Rams. He was the first out player drafted in the NFL, but he was cut before playing a single pro game. With no other options in the NFL, Sam became the first openly gay player in the Canadian Football League. He played a few games for the Montreal Alouettes in 2015 before retiring that year, citing mental health reasons.

Since then, there's been a gap, with no Big Four players coming out in recent years. Why?

One theory is that being gay would damage their careers. How would their teammates react? Would they be passed over in a draft or lose a contract? Get less playing time from their coaches? Would fans refuse to watch? Then there are endorsement opportunities to consider.

"A job in the NHL is so lucrative, and sometimes so short-lived, that the idea of getting media attention or perhaps feeling like you need to be a spokesperson is not worth it," says Cheryl MacDonald, citing her research on homophobia in hockey.

In short, Big Four athletes have not wanted to be distracted. Or be a distraction. Being "the gay player" just hasn't been seen as worth the risk.

Brian Burke — Paving the way for Inclusion in the NHL

Few causes are more important to former NHL general manager Brian Burke than fighting homophobia in sports. Burke's son, Brendan, came out in 2009. Brendan told his family there was a lot of discrimination in hockey. Brendan died in a car crash a few months later. In response to this tragedy, the whole Burke family got together to find a way to make sure Brendan would be remembered. That's how You Can Play was created.

When Brian Burke goes to schools to talk to kids about ending homophobia in sports, he tells them they need to take three steps as a group:

1. Practise acceptance. This isn't just tolerance, it's full acceptance and equality.
2. Stop bullying. Intervene if you see it. Report it if it's implied.
3. Take a positive step on behalf of the LGBTQ+ community. Join an organization, donate, march. Do something. Don't just say it.

Brian Burke (second from right) marches in Pride Parades and is active with an organization called Parents, Families and Friends of Lesbians and Gays (PFLAG).

Thanks to organizations that promote inclusion in sport, including You Can Play, some progress is being made — especially in the NHL. Each NHL team now hosts a Hockey Is for Everyone night. Fans can buy pride tape and rainbow jerseys on the NHL's website. Even the players tape their sticks and wear rainbow warm-up jerseys to show the world that hockey should include everyone.

When Cheryl MacDonald interviewed minor hockey players for her research, they said they are open to having a gay teammate. She also found that the team culture changed when a gay player came out. Teammates became more sensitive about the jokes they made in the locker room. According to her, education and visibility are the keys to progress.

As a #OneTeam ambassador, Brock McGillis shares his painful experiences with kids across the country. He explains how the homophobic hockey culture made him want to kill himself. He tells them how he was so afraid to be himself that he dated women. He felt suicidal and depressed. Often, he suffered from season-ending injuries. He wanted to be accepted, but he was too afraid to come out. "It feels empty. Hollow inside," he wrote on the Canadian Olympic Team website. "You think that you will never be able to live a happy, comfortable life as yourself and be involved in hockey."

Things changed for Brock when he came out. Now, he offers a hopeful message. "Keep pushing through," he wrote. "You may not feel comfortable coming out right now — that's okay. One day, trust me, you will come out and it will feel liberating. You will persevere."

Timeline

LGBTQ+ Rights in Canada

Prepared by Sandra Kirby, Ph.D., and Guylaine Demers, Ph.D.

1918: North America's first LGBTQ+ magazine is published in Montreal in secret.

1950–1970: The Royal Canadian Mounted Police (RCMP) tracks homosexuals in gay bars in cities in Canada. They also alert the Federal Bureau of Investigation (FBI) when suspected homosexuals cross the border with the United States.

1964: *Maclean's* magazine publishes "The Homosexual Next Door," the first positive article about LGBTQ+ Canadians.

June 29, 1969: The Government of Canada decriminalizes homosexuality.

1973: Pride Week 1973 is a national event that is held in several Canadian cities including Toronto, Vancouver, Ottawa, Montreal, Saskatoon and Winnipeg.

1974: Canada's first same-sex marriage takes place between Chris Vogel and Richard North of Winnipeg.

March 4, 1974: In Ottawa, several gay men's identities are made public after they are arrested and charged. At least one man, Warren Zufelt, commits suicide.

1976: In the lead up to the Summer Olympic Games, Montreal's mayor, Jean Drapeau, cracks downs on the city's gay village in an attempt to "clean up" the city. Public protests result.

December 1977: Quebec passes a law banning discrimination on the basis of sexual orientation.

February 5, 1981: Police raid four bath houses in Toronto. The community protests in what is now recognized as the first Toronto Pride event.

1982: Betty Baxter, coach and former star of the national women's volleyball team, is fired for being a lesbian.

1988: British Columbian Svend Robinson comes out, becoming Canada's first elected member of Parliament to be openly gay.

August 4, 1990: Vancouver hosts the 1990 Gay Games. It is the largest sporting event in the world that year.

October 16, 1993: *The Inside Track*, a documentary series on CBC, airs the episode "The Last Closet" about homophobia in sport. The disguised voices of two athletes, later identified as Mark Leduc and Mark Tewksbury, are part of the program.

1995: The Supreme Court of Canada rules that sexual orientation is protected under the *Canadian Charter of Rights and Freedoms*.

December 1998: Olympic gold medallist Mark Tewksbury comes out as gay after losing a six-figure contract as a motivational speaker because he is "too gay."

September 1999: In Winnipeg, the night before the opening of the Pan American Games, the International Olympic Committee (IOC) ends mandatory gender testing of all athletes entered in women's events.

June 10, 2003: The Ontario Court of Appeal determines that the definition of marriage as being between one man and one woman violates section 15 of the *Canadian Charter of Rights and Freedoms*. Within two years, same-sex marriage becomes legal in many provinces and one territory.

July 22, 2006: Transgender athlete Michelle Dumaresq wins the national mountain bike championships. When Dumaresq stands on the podium to accept her medal, second-place winner Danika Schroeter mocks her with *100% Pure Woman Champ 2006* written on her shirt.

July 26, 2006: Mark Tewksbury hosts the 2006 World OutGames in Montreal.

February 8, 2010: The Vancouver 2010 Winter Olympic Games begin and the first ever Pride House for LGBTQ+ athletes is located at Whistler, British Columbia.

October 14, 2011: Fifteen-year-old figure skater Jamie Hubley commits suicide after being bullied for being gay. The Ontario government announces that schools will have stiffer penalties for bullying and dedicates the It Gets Better Project to Hubley's memory.

March 4, 2012: You Can Play is launched to promote inclusiveness in sport.

February 11, 2013: Kathleen Wynne becomes Canada's first openly LGBTQ+ first minister and premier of Ontario.

March 20, 2013: Bill C-279, which extends humans rights protections to transgender and transsexual people, is passed.

August 16, 2013: The *Toronto Star* reports that current anti-gay laws in Russia might make life difficult for some athletes at the 2014 Sochi Olympic Games.

December 2, 2014: The Canadian Olympic Committee (COC) announces a partnership with You Can Play and Egale Canada Human Rights Trust (Egale) to create a more LGBTQ+ inclusive environment within the Canadian Olympic Team and COC's corporate offices.

December 2014: *Outsports* magazine publishes profiles of three openly gay Canadian Olympians: Kris Burley, Rosie Cossar and Eric Radford.

July 15, 2015: First Pan American Games Pride House for LGBTQ+ athletes is organized in Toronto.

June 1, 2016: For the first time, the Government of Canada raises the Pride flag on Parliament Hill.

January 11, 2018: Jessica Platt announces that she is transgender, becoming the first transgender woman to come out in the Canadian Women's Hockey League (CWHL).

February 2018: Canadian pairs skater, Eric Radford, becomes the first openly gay man to win a gold medal (in the skating team event) at a Winter Olympic Games in PyeongChang.

References:

Kirby, S.L. in Mountjoy et al, 2016 IOC Consensus Statement

Wikipedia.org, "Timeline of LGBT History in Canada"

Glossary

Ally: A person who believes in the dignity and respect of all people and takes action by supporting and advocating with groups being targeted by social injustice.

Anti-gay laws in Russia: Russia's policies on LGBTQ+ rights were a major concern leading up to the Sochi Winter Games in 2014. That's because in 2012 a Russian court blocked the establishment of a Pride House in Sochi for the games because it would "contradict" public morality. In June 2013, Russia was criticized around the world after it passed a federal gay propaganda law that made it a criminal offence to distribute materials considered "propaganda of non-traditional sexual relationships" among minors. In other words, it was illegal to be openly gay.

Big Four sports: This term refers to the biggest male professional sports leagues in North America. These sports have the highest revenue and the most fans, and their athletes often become icons. These leagues include the National Football League (NFL), the National Basketball League (NBA), Major League Baseball (MLB) and the National Hockey League (NHL). Major League Soccer (MLS) is also popular.

Bisexual: A sexual orientation in which gender is not a determining factor in sexual feelings toward another person.

Canadian Association for the Advancement of Women and Sport and Physical Activity (now called Canadian Women & Sport): Established in 1981, this is a national non-profit organization dedicated to creating an equitable sport and physical activity system where girls and women are participants and leaders. CWS offers many services, programs and resources to sport and physical activity organizations, teachers, coaches, athletes, volunteers and health and recreation professionals. They work with government and non-government organizations in activities and initiatives that advocate for positive change for girls and women in sport and physical activity and to make sport more welcoming to those who are LGBTQ+ (womenandsport.ca).

Canadian Olympic Committee (COC): The Canadian Olympic Committee is the private, non-profit organization that represents Canada at the International Olympic Committee (IOC). The COC works with national sports federations to prepare Team Canada for the Olympic Games, Youth Olympic Games and Pan American Games. The COC also manages several cultural and educational programs promoting Olympic values in Canada and selects and supports Canadian cities when they want to host the Olympics and Pan American Games (olympic.ca and paralympic.ca).

Cisgender: Cisgender (or cis) is a gender identity term that describes people whose gender identity matches their biological sex at birth. For example, someone who identifies herself as a woman and is born biologically female is a cisgender woman.

Coming out/being out or out of the closet: The process of becoming aware of your sexual orientation or gender identity and sharing this identity with others. Being "outed" is when a person's sexual or gender identity is revealed without permission to someone else, leaving the "outed" person feeling vulnerable and at risk.

Egale Canada Human Rights Trust (Egale Canada): Egale's vision is a Canada, and ultimately a world, without homophobia, biphobia, transphobia and all other forms of oppression, in which every person can achieve their full potential, free from hatred and bias. Egale informs public policy, inspires cultural change and promotes human rights and inclusion through research, education and community engagement (egale.ca).

Gay: A way to describe sexual orientation of those who are attracted to people of the same gender. It's often used to describe only men who are sexually attracted to men.

Hockey Is for Everyone: An NHL slogan that refers to the idea that the NHL supports any teammate, coach or fan who brings heart, energy and passion to the rink. Their goal is to ensure the sport is a positive and inclusive environment for players, their families and fans of every race, colour, religion, national origin, gender, age, sexual orientation and socio-economic status and for those with disabilities.

Homophobia: A term describing a range of negative feelings toward lesbian and gay people as individuals or as a group. Homophobia can show itself as hateful or insulting language or actions, even violence, directed toward lesbian and gay people or those assumed to be lesbian or gay.

Intersex: A person whose chromosomal, hormonal, or anatomical sex characteristics fall outside of the conventional classifications of male or female.

Lesbian: A way to describe the sexual orientation of women who are sexually attracted to women.

LGBTQ+: An initialism for lesbian, gay, bisexual, trans, queer and other sexually and gender-diverse minorities, including intersex and two-spirit identities.

Locker room culture: The locker room can be a vulnerable place where close bonding with teammates occurs. Anxiety or fear about being labelled gay can lead some athletes to "prove" their heterosexuality by using anti-gay language or talking about sexual activity with the opposite sex. Some LGBTQ+ coaches and athletes are uncomfortable in the locker room because they are concerned about how others perceive them.

#OneTeam ambassador: The #OneTeam Athlete Ambassador Program organizes Olympians across Canada to talk about mental health and equality in sport. Ambassadors include LGBTQ+ athletes and straight allies. The program is a partnership of the Canadian

Olympic Committee, You Can Play and Egale Canada. They are working together to ensure all LGBTQ+ athletes, coaches and fans feel safe and included in sports, both on and off the field.

Out on the Fields: Released in 2015, *Out on the Fields* was the first and largest international study on homophobia in sports. Nearly 9,500 people participated, including 1,123 lesbian, gay, bisexual and straight Canadians. The study focused on team sports and sexuality in English-speaking countries and was reviewed by an international panel of experts. The results showed homophobia to be present at all levels of sport and reinforced the need for more work to be done to ensure everyone feels safe in sport (outonthefields.com).

Pride House: Pride House hosts LGBTQ+ athletes, coaches, volunteers and visitors during the Olympics, Paralympics or other international sporting events in the host city. The first Pride House was organized for the Vancouver 2010 Winter Olympics.

Testosterone: This is a male sex hormone related to the development of certain characteristics in men, including sperm production, a deeper voice, hair production, the creation of blood cells and muscle mass. There has been no conclusive proof, however, that higher levels of testosterone alone give athletes an advantage in physical performance.

The Gay Games: The Gay Games were first held in 1982 as the Gay Olympics, designed to promote the spirit of inclusion and participation, as well as to promote the pursuit of personal growth. In Europe, the European Gay and Lesbian Sport Federation organizes the EuroGames. With more than 8,000 participants, the first World Out Games in 2006 was the largest international sporting event to be held in Montreal since the 1976 Summer Olympics.

Transgender: A gender identity term that describes a person who is assigned the male or female sex at birth but identifies as a different sex.

Transitioning: The process by which a trans man or woman lives as the gender they identify with. It can include changing their name, gender identity and clothes, and possibly medical treatments like hormone therapy or gender confirming surgery. Transitioning is a complicated process that varies from person to person and can take many years.

You Can Play: You Can Play was launched in 2012 in honour of Brendan Burke, who died in a car crash in 2009 after coming out. You Can Play is involved in a number of initiatives to help all LGBTQ+ athletes, coaches and fans feel safe and included in sports. Their goal is to ensure teams focus on an athlete's skills and work ethic rather than their sexual orientation and/or gender identity (youcanplayproject.org).

Acknowledgements

I'd like to thank all the athletes who spoke with me for this book. It's such an important topic and I was honoured to share their stories. These athletes work hard, not only to excel in sport, but to be role models for others. Their willingness to share their experiences and give their time has, no doubt, made a big difference in the lives of countless schoolchildren and young athletes. They are all an inspiration and doing such great work to promote inclusiveness at all levels of sport. I'm also thankful for the amazing photos they shared.

Thanks to Kat and Carrie and the team at Lorimer for giving me the chance to bring this book to fruition. I appreciate all the time they spent helping me make this book the best it could be. The reason I became a writer was to make a difference. I hope this book is meaningful for readers.

Thank you also to the folks at the Canadian Olympic Committee and to Brian Burke with You Can Play for their interest in this project. Also to Jennifer-Birch Jones at CWS and Dennis Quesnel at Egale who read through the manuscript and suggested so many meaningful edits. With their support, I hope we can continue to spread the message of inclusiveness. Sport should be a welcoming place for everyone. All their great initiatives are helping accomplish this important mission.

I want to thank my Brian Henry writing group for reading my manuscript and offering their honest advice. Brian and everyone else in the group helped make this a better book. I have always looked forward to our Friday morning discussions.

I couldn't have gotten this far without the support of my family. I especially want to mention my husband, Scott, my best friend, Danya, and my parents, Michael and Judy. Their encouragement helped me press ahead when I wanted to give up. From offering feedback and advice to reading my chapters, I will always be grateful for their love and support.

I dedicate this book to my boys, Josh and Ari. They are the funniest, most clever kids I know and they have more energy than I can often handle! I am so proud to be their mom — I hope my perseverance makes them proud of me, too. And to my stepdaughter, Daniella, the biggest cheerleader and most voracious reader in the family.

I also dedicate this book to every child who has ever been bullied or discriminated against for being who they are. I hope in some way this book helps make the world a safer place.

Photo Credits

Page 8, 10: Courtesy of Mark Tewksbury

Page 12–13, 15, 41: Courtesy of the Canadian Olympic Committee, photos by Ted Grant

Page 16: Courtesy of Mark Tewksbury, photo by Lucas Murnaghan

Page 18: Alamy Stock Photo/UPI/Roger L. Wollenberg

Page 20: Courtesy of Anastasia Bucsis

Page 23: Courtesy of the Canadian Olympic Committee, photo by Jenna Muirhead-Gould

Page 25: Courtesy of Anastasia Bucsis, photo by David J. Phillip

Page 27: Courtesy of Scott MacArthur

Page 28, 33: Courtesy of Rose Cossar, photos by Bernard Theirolf

Page 30: Courtesy of Rose Cossar

Page 34: Courtesy of Rose Cossar, photo by Adam Pulicicchio

Page 35: Courtesy of the Canadian Olympic Committee, photo by Scott Grant

Page 36, 42: Courtesy of the Canadian Olympic Committee, photo by Jason Ransom

Page 38: Courtesy of Eric Radford

Page 39: Courtesy of the Canadian Olympic Committee, photo by David Jackson

Page 44: Courtesy of the Canadian Olympic Committee, photo by Adam Pulicicchio

Page 46: Courtesy of Betty Baxter

Page 50: Courtesy of Sophie Woodrooffe, photo by *The Tyee*

Page 51: Courtesy of Joey Lye, photo by John Kovac

Page 53: Courtesy of Joey Lye, photo by Jess Gowans

Page 54: Courtesy of the Canadian Olympic Committee, photo by Jeffrey Sze

Page 56: Courtesy of Cindy Ouellet, photo by Scott Grant

Page 58: Courtesy of Cindy Ouellet

Page 59: Courtesy of the Canadian Paralympic Committee, photo by Nicole Latreille

Page 62: Courtesy of the Canadian Paralympic Committee and Dominique Ladouceur, Agence AF-2

Page 64: Matthew Manor/Hockey Hall of Fame

Page 67: Courtesy of the Canadian Olympic Committee, photo by Winston Chow

Page 68, 70: Courtesy of Caroline Ouellette

Page 71: Courtesy of Caroline Ouellette, photo by Louis-Charles Dumais

Page 72, 74: Courtesy of Chris Voth, photos by Great Photo

Page 77: Courtesy of Chris Voth, photo by Francois Laplante/Freestyle Photography

Page 78, 82: Courtesy of Jessica Platt, photos by Chris Tanouye

Page 80: Courtesy of Jessica Platt

Page 83: Courtesy of Jessica Platt, photo by Lori Bolliger

Page 84: Courtesy of Chris Mosier, photo by Phil Lee

Page 87: Courtesy of Rachel McKinnon, photo by Craig Huffman Photography

Page 88, 91: Courtesy of Brock McGillis

Page 93: Courtesy of the Canadian Olympic Committee

Index

519, The, 28

Auch, Susan, 19

Balmertown, ON, 37, 45

baseball, 51, 90–91, 99

basketball, 91, 99
 wheelchair, 56, 58–63

Baxter, Betty, 46–50, 53, 96

Bill C-279, 97

Black Hockey and Sports Hall of Fame, 64

Brooks, AB, 46

Browne, Harrison, 83–84, 86

Bucknell University (Pennsylvania), 51, 53–54

Bucsis, Anastasia, 18–26

bullying, 9, 62, 93, 97

Burke, Brendan, 48, 93, 103

Burke, Brian, 26, 48, 93

Burley, Kris, 35, 98

Calgary, AB, 8, 18–19, 22

Canada, homophobia, 11

Canadian Association for the Advancement of Women in Sport (now called Canadian Women & Sport), 46, 50, 55, 99–100

Canadian Broadcasting Corporation (CBC), 8, 18, 20, 25, 90, 96

Canadian Centre for Gender and Sexuality, 28

Canadian Charter of Rights and Freedoms, 96–97

Canadian Olympic Committee (COC), 17, 23, 32, 34, 44, 48, 98, 100–1

Canadian Olympic Hall of Fame, 13

Canadian Olympic Team, 94, 98

Canadian Sports Hall of Fame, 13, 64

Canadian Wheelchair Basketball League (CWBL), 56

Canadian Women's Hockey League (CWHL), 65, 70, 78, 82–83, 98

cancer, 57–58, 62

Chu, Julie, 26, 69–71

Cirque du Soleil, 35

coaching, 7, 17, 32, 37, 40, 45–55, 69–71, 77, 84, 96, 101–3

Collins, Jason, 91

coming out, 15–16, 21–22, 27, 32, 38–41, 43, 48, 52, 55, 58, 67, 73–74, 76, 84, 91–94, 100

Cossar, Rosie, 26, 28–35, 98

criminalizing homosexuality, 95–96

depression, 14, 20–21, 24, 79, 94

Duhamel, Meagan, 38–39, 42–43

Dumaresq, Michelle, 97

Egale Canada, 17, 48, 98, 100–101

figure skating, 19, 35–45, 97

Gay Games, 46, 50, 96, 102

gymnastics, 19, 35, 41
    rhythmic, 28–34

hockey, 23, 26, 35, 48, 51, 64–72, 79–84, 88–94, 98–99, 101

Hockey Hall of Fame, 64, 66

homophobia in sport, 11, 15–16, 18, 24, 26–27, 30–32, 44, 47–49, 66, 73, 90–94, 96, 102

Hubley, Jamie, 97

Inside Out: Straight Talk from a Gay Jock, 10

International Olympic Committee, 32, 85, 96, 100

International Skating Union (ISU), 18, 36

International Swimming Hall of Fame, 14

intersectionality, 61

James, Angela, 64–67

Jordan-Young, Rebecca M., 86

Karkazis, Katrina, 86

Labonté, Charline, 23, 67

Leading the Way: Working with LGBTQ Athletes and Coaches, 55

Le May Doan, Catriona, 19

Lethbridge, AB, 9

locker-room homophobia, 16–17, 79, 89–91, 94, 101

Lye, Joey, 51–55

MacArthur, Scott, 27

MacDonald, Cheryl, 90, 92, 94

Major League Soccer (MLS), 48, 99

McGillis, Brock, 88–91, 94

McKinnon, Rachel, 87

mental health, 17, 20–21, 24, 26, 31, 92, 101

Montreal, QC, 17, 68, 81, 92, 95, 97, 102

Mosier, Chris, 83–84

Muhammad Ali Humanitarian Award for Gender Equality, 8

music, 36, 45, 57, 63

namecalling, *see* bullying

National Football League (NFL), 48, 91–92, 99

National Hockey League (NHL), 48, 90–94, 99, 101

New Democratic Party, 46

Oakville, ON, 27

Olympic Games, 8
    Barcelona (1992), 8, 11, 13
    history, 17
    homophobia in, 22, 24, 30, 85–86, 96
    London (2012), 28, 31, 63
    Montreal (1976), 48, 95
    PyeongChang (2018), 36, 41, 63, 98
    Salt Lake City (2002), 68
    Seoul (1988), 8, 11, 63

Sochi (2014), 18, 22, 24–25, 32, 36, 43, 68, 97, 99
    Turin (2006), 68
    Vancouver (2010), 18, 43, 68, 97, 102
#OneTeam initiative, 17, 23–24, 33, 35, 44–45, 94, 101
Ontario Hockey League, 72, 88
Ontario Sports Hall of Fame, 64
openly LGBT athletes, 15, 22, 39, 43, 49, 52, 55, 66, 73–75, 79, 83–84, 91–92, 98–99
Orser, Brian, 40–41
Ouellet, Cindy, 56–63
Ouellette, Caroline, 26, 68–71
Out in the Fields (report), 11
Outsports magazine, 35, 39, 41, 98
Out There Winnipeg, 76–77
Pan American Games, 28, 51, 96, 98, 100
Paralympic Games, 17, 56, 102
    Beijing (2008), 60
    history, 63
    London (2012), 61
    PyeongChang (2018), 61
    Rio (2016), 61, 84
    Vancouver (2010), 43
Parents, Families and Friends of Lesbians and Gays (PFLAG), 93
Platt, Jessica, 78–86, 98
Player's Own Voice (podcast), 14, 18, 25

Pride House, 43, 49, 97–99, 102
pride parades/events, 22, 26, 34, 76, 93, 95–96
public speaking, 8, 14, 34, 88
Queen's Medals, 8, 56
Radford, Eric, 36–45, 63, 98
Rivière-du-Loup, QC, 56–57
Robinson, Svend, 96
Rogers, Robbie, 92
role model, being a, 7, 15, 17, 22, 28, 33, 38, 49, 53, 71, 76, 82–83, 88
Rouse, Jeff, 12–13
same-sex marriage, 26, 52, 66, 69–71, 95
Sam, Michael, 92
Sarnia, ON, 78
school-based homophobia (*bully*), 9–10, 37, 47
secrets, keeping, 7, 10, 14, 16, 19, 29, 31, 40, 47–49, 52
skiing, para Nordic, 56, 61
softball, 51–55
Soulmates on Ice: From Hometown Glory to Top of the Podium, 36
speed skating, 18–26
Sports Illustrated, 91
Sportsnet, 27, 37–38
Standing on the Line (documentary), 18
stereotypes, 75–76
Student-Athlete Mental Health Initiative (SAMHI), 20

Sudbury, ON, 88

suicide, 21, 94, 95, 97

support, 21, 27, 32, 39–43, 55, 58, 68–70, 76, 81, 84, 86, 93–94

    lack of, 21–22, 27, 32, 52

swimming, 8–17

    para-, 58

Team Canada, 26, 28, 51, 53–54, 60, 63, 67, 100

testosterone in sport, 85–86

Tewksbury, Mark, 8–17, 22, 26, 43, 96–97

Todd, Sugar, 25

Toronto, ON, 51, 64–65, 95–96, 98

Toronto Furies, 78, 82–83

Toronto Star, 17, 59–60, 97

track and field, 86

    para-, 58

transgender rights advocacy, 78, 82–83, 87

transphobia in sport, 84–85, 87, 97

University of Alabama, 60–61

University of Calgary, 10, 17–18, 25

University of Ottawa, 48

University of Southern California, 63

volleyball, 46–50, 72–77, 96

Voth, Chris, 72–77

Wilfrid Laurier University, 81

Winnipeg, MB, 36, 72, 76–77, 95

Winnipeg Free Press, 73

Wirtz, Paul, 37

World Baseball Softball Confederation (WBSC), 51

World Cup, 18, 24

World Rhythmic Gymnastics Championships, 28

World OutGames, 17, 97

Wynne, Kathleen, 97

You Can Play (YCP), 17, 24, 26, 48–49, 70, 84, 86, 93–94, 97–98, 101, 103

Zeigler, Cyd, 41